012881144

D0364710

A

SOCIOMETRY AND EDUCATION

INTERNATIONAL LIBRARY OF SOCIOLOGY
AND SOCIAL RECONSTRUCTION

Founded by Karl Mannheim

Editor: W. J. H. Sprott

A catalogue of the books available in the INTERNATIONAL LIBRARY OF SOCIOLOGY AND SOCIAL RECONSTRUCTION, and new books in preparation for the Library, will be found at the end of this volume.

SOCIOMETRY
AND EDUCATION

by

K. M. EVANS

B.Sc., M.A., Ph.D. (Lond.)

Lecturer and Research Officer in Educational Psychology
Faculty of Education, University College of
South Wales and Monmouthshire

LONDON
ROUTLEDGE & KEGAN PAUL
NEW YORK: THE HUMANITIES PRESS

First published 1962
by Routledge and Kegan Paul Ltd.
Broadway House, 68-74 Carter Lane
London, E.C.4

Printed in Great Britain
by Lowe & Brydone (Printers) Ltd, London

Second impression 1966

CONTENTS

v

PREFACE

STUDENTS of sociometry in Britain have often felt themselves handicapped by the relative inaccessibility of many of the journals and theses in which accounts of the work in this field are to be found. Books on the subject are mainly American and references in them to the growing body of British sociometric studies are few. This book is an attempt to give an account of the main sociometric techniques, to show how they can be used and the results interpreted, and to synthesize some of the information obtained by applying them in the classroom. It draws on British as well as American sources.

The author would like to take this opportunity of acknowledging generous help received from the Library Staff of the University College of South Wales and Monmouthshire in tracing sources, from the students and teachers who have shown a keen interest in sociometry, and from Dr. C. M. Fleming, who encouraged the writing of this book and read and commented on the manuscript. Without this help the book could never have been written.

Cardiff, 1961

vii

I

THE FORMATION OF GROUPS

IN recent years awareness has been growing of the influence exerted on the behaviour and development of human beings by the groups to which they belong. Very few people live in complete isolation from their fellows, and the normal individual in our society is a member of a variety of groups, most of which are small. Indeed the fundamental social unit is a small group, the family.

For very young children life is bounded by the family, but as they grow older and go out into the world they become aware of their membership of a wider society composed of fellow-villagers or citizens, fellow-countrymen, the whole human race. Nevertheless most people continue to function as members of small groups rather than as members of the wider society. A child is a member of his class at school before he realizes himself as a member of the school, and his school life is lived mainly in his classroom with only brief excursions into the assembly of the whole school. Later, as an adult, he may become an employee of a firm or organization, but he lives his working life in a workshop or office group. In his leisure hours he may be a member of a team or social group, and if he belongs to a Church he actually lives his Church life as a member of the local congregation, and is probably more aware of this membership than of the wider Church of which it forms a part. If he falls sick, he may find himself among a group of people in a hospital ward or in some other kind of therapeutic group. In old age he may return to the shelter of his family group or he may seek refuge in a home for old people. From the cradle to the grave we are members of small groups.

At this point it becomes necessary to give some definition of what is meant by a group. In one sense any aggregate of people may be called a group, but it is usual to distinguish between two types of situation in which people may be found together. The first might be represented by the passengers in a bus, who may not know one another or have anything in common except that they are travelling along the same route at the same time. They have no common purpose, and no role or status relationships towards one another. Such a situation is described as a 'togetherness situation' rather than as a 'group situation'. It can be contrasted with the situation where a number of people come together as members of, say, a tennis club. Here there is a common purpose, to play tennis, and the members have definite role and status relationships towards one another, whether as committee or team members or as partners or opponents in a friendly game. There are rules of membership and of tennis which are accepted by the individual members and by which they are bound in their activities in the club, and they see themselves and are seen by others to be bound together and set apart from non-members. Such an aggregate would be regarded as a true group. Sherif and Sherif (1956) have defined a group as 'a social unit which consists of a number of individuals who stand in (more or less) definite status and role relationships to one another and which possesses a set of values or norms of its own regulating the behavior of individual members, at least in matters of consequence to the group'.

A class of children in a school differs in some respects from either the people in a bus or the members of a tennis club. To begin with, the children are not in school entirely of their own free will. They are there because the law of the land says that children of their age must attend school and their parents have complied with the law and sent them there. In school they have been allocated to a particular class according to some criterion such as age, sex, intelligence, attainment, or the initial letters of their surnames. They are thus together, in the first place, by

2

compulsion, and though they are at school for a purpose the purpose may not be theirs, and it may, indeed, be one of which their parents do not approve. Certainly parents do not all have the same reasons for sending their children to school. From this it appears that the children in a school class are together but are not, in the strict sense, a group. This is true generally when the children first enter the class as strangers to one another. It is possible, however, for a togetherness situation to develop into a group situation, and this is what usually happens in a school class. The children work and play together for several hours a day, and as a result they develop relationships of role and status among themselves and common attitudes towards outsiders as represented by teachers, children in other classes and other schools. A class of children who have been together for any length of time may be regarded as a group in any but the most abnormal circumstances.

Within a class it is usually possible to observe a number of more or less well-developed subgroups. These are friendship groups. At first, and among young children, they are often friendship pairs. These develop among older children into larger groups which change both in membership and internal structure. The structure of adolescent groups is likely to be much more complex than that of groups of younger children, and is likely to show an awareness of sexual differences and attractions which is not usually to be observed at earlier ages.

Several factors contribute to the formation of children's groups. Partridge (1943) has suggested that propinquity is basic in group formation. Children who live in the same neighbourhood and go to the same school tend to play together and often, as in the case reported by Kerstetter (1940), to sit and work together in school. Evans and Wilson (1949) found that among women university students also, friends were chosen from those whose rooms were in proximity in a hall of residence. Giddens (1960) made a similar observation among men students.

Social nearness is also a factor in friendship formation and Potashin (1946) has observed that children seem to make friends with others of the same social class. It is possible that this may merely be another aspect of propinquity, since the

3

people living in any neighbourhood are likely to be of nearly the same social class, and family friendships are usually within a social class. Thus children tend to meet more children of their own social class than they do of those from other classes. Hallworth (1952) found that among children in a grammar school the spontaneous groups formed were associated with value-systems, and again it is true that value-systems vary from one social class to another. Children may therefore tend to choose friends from their own social class because they meet more of them and have similar value-systems.

Common play interests were noted by Partridge (1943) as a basis for group formation. Here again there may be a value-system involved. He also reported that adolescent groups frequently formed and were perpetuated in response to adult antagonism and suppression. Another value-system seems to operate here, as it does also in the case of groups of young people whose aim is social usefulness. Wolman (1958) wrote: 'A group is what it is to its members. How it is perceived by the members and what their motivations about the group are determine its nature.'

Hallworth (1952) made some interesting observations on the way in which the internal structure of groups developed as time went on. He found that groups which began as small, loosely-knit structures tended to become larger and better integrated. They were centred round four or five individuals of whom one tended to be over-chosen. The 'central core' represented values recognized by the members and often as many as two-thirds of the choices of the whole group were directed to the 'central core'. As the group became better integrated and more stable more and more choices tended to go to the 'central core', but the tendency for them to be centred on one individual decreased and they became spread instead over several individuals. This normal course of development was sometimes hindered where there was no suitable personality round whom the group could form, and in this case there was instead a constantly changing pattern of small groups.

A very similar state of affairs was found by Pearce (1958). He observed that when the more able boys, who were also the

4

leaders, were removed from a form in a grammar school, the structure of the form was destroyed. These boys evidently personified the values of the rest, and no others could take their place. As a result of their removal the group disintegrated. Shears (1952), working with more able children of the same age, found that when the original leaders were removed from a class, others took their place, but that there did come a point where, after the repeated removal of leaders, the group did not reform. All this is evidence for the thesis that groups do, in fact, form around individuals who personify the values of the members.

It is found that where boys and girls are thrown together there is a tendency during later childhood and early adolescence for single-sex subgroups to form. Partridge (1943) observed that during adolescence girls seemed less disposed than boys to form spontaneous groups. This may be because boys and girls at some ages have different value-systems, which may, in turn, be a result of their different rates of maturing and of the different roles for which they are cast by nature and by the larger society.

Sherif and Sherif (1956) listed four essential properties of small informal groups.

1. *Common motives conducive to interaction*
Informal groups come into being where a number of individuals who have common motives and goals interact. These motives and goals may be the result of common needs and ambitions, interests and attitudes, fears and dangers. In a class of children interest in games, rebellion against authority, a liking for a particular teacher, or common hobby are among the motives which may lead to the formation of groups. It should be noted, though, that strong common emotions such as rivalry, ambition, or fear of punishment may disrupt a group.

2. *Differential effects of interaction on members*
When individuals react with one another changes occur in their thinking, emotional reactions and behaviour. These can be related to the organization and standards of the group, and it is observable that the effects are different for different individuals. These depend on the role and status relationships between the members of the groups.

5

3. *Formation of group structure*
One result of association in groups is that the members develop role and status relationships towards one another. The role of an individual refers to the behaviour expected of him by other members of the group. The status of an individual is the position which he occupies in the hierarchy of the group by reason of any abilities or capacities which he may possess. There is a range of behaviour which will be tolerated for any individual by the group members, and when a stable group structure has evolved the individual adopts as his own the standards and values of the group.

4. *Formation of group norms*
In any group with a stable structure definite norms of behaviour can be observed. These may be in the form of slang and nicknames, customs and ritual, and reactions to members of other groups. The secret societies which flourish in late childhood and early adolescence are examples of this. So are the gangs whose codes of honour are usually strict and often conflict with adult codes. Deviation from the group norm may on occasion be visited with very severe penalties or even with expulsion from the group.

The extent to which a group can influence the behaviour of an individual will depend on the degree to which he is attracted to it. According to Lewin (1947), most people adopt standards which are very close to those of a group to which they wish to belong, and put up considerable resistance towards moving away from the standards of socially valuable groups. Indeed, he asserted that groups are often more pliable than individuals, and that it is usually easier to change individuals formed into a group than to change any one of them separately. Smith (1946) found that over a period of several years during which he studied the attitudes of students in sociology classes to such subjects as the treatment of criminals, the Negro question and birth control, where a statistically significant change of attitude took place there was also an increase in homogeneity of attitude. Lewin (1947) says that one way to change the attitude of individuals is to diminish the strength of the value of the group standard which is perceived by the individuals as having social value.

Rasmussen and Zander (1954) noted that group standards tend to serve as levels of aspiration for their members, and that lack of conformity to the group norms, in so far as it is perceived as non-achievement of an ideal level of performance, provokes

6

feelings of failure, whereas conformity is equivalent to achievement and induces feelings of success. The feeling of success or failure is more or less strong according to the individual's attraction to the group and the apparent importance of the issues to the group. Comparisons of the self with other members of an admired group were shown by Festinger, Torrey and Willerman (1954) to contribute to the individual's sense of his own adequacy or inadequacy.

Recognition of the influence of groups on individuals has led in recent years to an increasing emphasis on the study of groups as opposed to the study of individuals. This has been particularly true in the field of education and an excellent account of the steps by which we have come to realize that 'the teacher has never to do with an individual child in the sense of an entity with fixed attributes unfolding in comparative independence of the treatment he receives but always with a child within a group' has been given by Fleming (1955). This change of viewpoint has been accompanied by the search for and development of techniques for gathering and recording reliable data about the structure and development of groups, and between a group and its individual members. Of these techniques sociometry is one of the most interesting, as well as one of the most suitable for classroom use. Developed in America, its use is now becoming widespread in Britain, and Blyth (1960) has gathered together the results of a number of sociometric studies made in English schools.

In the ensuing pages an attempt is made to give an outline of sociometric techniques which, without claiming to be exhaustive, is sufficiently detailed to enable results obtained by these methods to be understood and critically appraised, and to give any who wish to experiment with them an indication of how they can be applied and the uses to which they can be put. This is followed by an account of some of the more important findings about groups of children and young people, mainly in school and recreational groups, and because no classroom group is complete without a teacher the relationships between teachers and pupils are also considered. Finally, there is a brief consideration of teachers as people and craftsmen, and of the skills involved in the art of teaching the young.

7

II

SOCIOMETRY AND THE SOCIO-
METRIC TEST

I. SOCIOMETRY AND ITS ORIGINS

THERE can be few subjects whose origins are as well-defined as are those of sociometry. The story of the development of the sociometric movement has been told both by its founder, J. L. Moreno (1953), and by Toeman (1949). The latter divided the history of the movement into three parts. The first part covered the years 1905-1925 when Moreno was still living and working in Europe, applying group therapy to children in Vienna, and developing his ideas of the interaction of persons. Between 1915 and 1918 Moreno was employed by the Austrian government to help with the organization of a colony of more than 10,000 Austrian citizens of Italian extraction, who fled from the South Tyrol before the Italian army and were resettled near Mittendorf, not far from Vienna. It was through his contacts with these people that he arrived at the idea of a sociometrically planned community, and it was in a letter which he wrote to the Austro-Hungarian Department of the Interior in 1916 that the word 'sociometry' was first used.

The second period began in 1925 when Moreno arrived in New York. Here he gathered a band of six helpers whose names he has recorded. They were William H. Bridge, E. Stagg Whitin, Helen H. Jennings, William Alanson White, Fanny French Morse and Gardner Murphy. In 1933, the Medical

Society of the State of New York held a convention at which Moreno read a paper on the experimental study of small groups entitled 'Psychological Organization of Groups in the Community'. This paper was illustrated by an exhibit of over a hundred sociometric charts, and these charts caught the imagination not only of the delegates but also of the press, and they received considerable publicity. In the following year, 1934, Moreno's book *Who Shall Survive? A New Approach to the Problem of Human Relations* was published, and it became what he has described as 'the foundation stone of the sociometric movement'.

There followed a period of consolidation during which much research was carried out and two journals made their appearance. The brief-lived *Sociometric Review* appeared in 1936 only to be replaced in 1937 by *Sociometry, A Journal of Interpersonal Relations*, whose first editor was Gardner Murphy.

The third period, which began in 1941, has seen the spread of sociometric ideas throughout the United States and to Europe and other parts of the world. In 1941 Beacon House, a publishing house for sociometric books and monographs, was founded. It issued in 1953 a much enlarged edition of *Who Shall Survive?* with the subtitle *Foundations of Sociometry, Group Psychotherapy and Sociodrama*.

The year 1942 saw the foundation of the Sociometric Institute in New York. The aims of the Institute included a school exclusively dedicated to the teaching of sociometric disciplines and the training of qualified sociometrists able to introduce courses in sociometry in their own universities. It was intended that the Institute should be a meeting-point of all the sciences in which it partakes: psychology, sociology, cultural anthropology, biology, psychiatry and economics. To aid in this work the Institute undertook responsibility for the expansion and improvement of *Sociometry*, and the publication both of books and monographs and of popularized statements designed to make the general public aware of the value of sociometry.

Acting on the assumption that 'the best way to spread a novel idea is to "give it away"' (Moreno, 1955a), Moreno in 1955 transferred the journal *Sociometry* to the American

Sociological Society. Since then its full title has been *Sociometry: A Journal of Research in Social Psychology*.

Sociometry and sociometrists have not been without their critics. Loomis and Pepinsky (1948) examined a large number of papers published in *Sociometry* and concluded that they have 'greatly enriched both our knowledge and understanding of social relationships and have contributed materially to our store of techniques for the investigation of interpersonal and intergroup phenomena'. At the same time they pointed out that there is a tendency to use esoteric terms which are intelligible only to the initiated and create barriers to communication. They recommended greater clarity of expression, more careful statements of purpose, assumptions and hypotheses, and more explicit statements with regard to basic data and the methods by which they are processed. Some of the mathematical techniques used have been criticized by Edwards (1948).

It may be considered that Moreno (1955b) made too high-sounding a claim when he wrote: 'The aim of sociometry is to help in the formation of a world in which every individual whatever his intelligence, race, creed, religion or ideological affiliations, is given an equal opportunity to survive and to apply his spontaneity and creativity within it.' It may also be questioned whether the realization of this aim would be good for society. Whatever one's views on this may be, one must agree with Lindzey and Borgatta (1954) that sociometric measures are now so widely used both by social psychologists and sociologists that some knowledge of sociometric techniques is necessary for anyone working in these areas.

What is sociometry? The term has been subjected to considerable criticism. From analogy with terms such as biometrics and psychometrics it might be considered to be concerned with the measurement of social behaviour. Both Moreno (1953) and others, such as Chapin (1940), have analysed the word sociometry into *socius*, translated by Moreno as *companion* and by Chapin as *social*, and either the Latin *metrum* or Greek *metron, a measure*. From this point on there appears to be a divergence of opinion, Moreno using the word in a narrower and Chapin using it in a wider sense.

Moreno has said that 'sociometry deals with the mathematical study of psychological properties of populations, the experimental technique of and the results obtained by the application of quantitative methods. This is undertaken through methods which inquire into the evolution and organization of groups and the position of individuals within them'. According to this definition, sociometry is concerned only with the social structure of groups and not with such topics as the measurement of attitudes, interests and personality qualities of the individuals who compose them.

Chapin, on the other hand, defined sociometrics as the 'study and use of social measurements'. He classified social measurements into three categories.

1. Psychometrics or psychological measurements.

2. Demogrametrics or measurements of large units of population.

3. Sociometrics, including (*a*) scales to measure the interaction process within social groups, and (*b*) those that attempt to measure the family group and the home environment.

It will be seen that Moreno's use of the word sociometry is confined to the third of Chapin's categories. It seems to be further restricted in practice to what Chapin described as 'procedures that attempt to measure informal friendship constellations and seem to get at the latent cultural patterns of a group of people'. This appears to be a very narrow field, but it cannot be denied that Moreno and his followers have developed effective instruments and techniques for its study and have been responsible for making available a considerable amount of interesting and useful material about the structure and development of groups, and about the ways in which these can be modified.

Several different approaches in sociometric work are mentioned by Moreno (1937). There is first a research procedure, in which the aim is to study the organization of a group or groups. Then there is a diagnostic procedure where the aim is to classify the positions of individuals in a group or of groups in a wider community. Thirdly, there is what may be either a therapeutic or political procedure aimed at helping individuals or groups to a better adjustment. Lastly, there is what Moreno calls the complete sociometric procedure where all these approaches are united. The instrument used to obtain the information needed for the application of any of these procedures is the sociometric test.

II. THE SOCIOMETRIC TEST

A sociometric test is designed to give an objective picture of the relationships existing between the members of any group of people. Its object is to bring to light the attractions and repulsions between the individual members and it is an extremely easy test to administer. The usual method is simply to ask each member of the group to indicate which other members he would like to have as companions for a particular activity or occasion, and also any he would dislike having as companions for that activity or occasion.

To facilitate the interpretation of the results the group from which the choices may be made should be delimited. If this is not done the individuals may spread their choices over the whole field of their acquaintance and the relationships within the group itself may not become apparent. Thus in dealing with children in school their choices may be confined to their own class and not allowed to spread to the whole school or to people whom they know outside the school. There is, however, a possibility that information may be required as to the extent to which free choices would be given within the group, and in that case the area of choice would not be restricted.

The activity or occasion for which companions are to be chosen should always be specified. Although there are groups of friends who choose to be together whatever the activity upon which they are engaged, it must be borne in mind that the most desirable companion for one activity may be less desirable for a different activity. One might choose to play a game with one person, attend a concert with a second, and collaborate in writing a book with a third.

Where the purpose of the test is to obtain information about a group the choice of a suitable criterion is important. As Borgatta (1951) pointed out, a teacher who constructs a sociogram after asking the class 'With whom would you like to sit?' 'has committed the fallacy of accepting a well-estab-

12

lished procedure without exploring her own needs as well as those of her class'. Consideration of the use to which the results are to be put should always precede the administration of the test and should determine the choice of criterion.

In order that the choices may be real it is desirable that the group should have been in existence for some time, so that the members know one another and the capacities and limitations of individuals, and real likes and dislikes have emerged. If the group is of recent formation the choices are likely to be superficial and based upon inadequate information or irrelevant factors, but this does not prevent choices being made, as was shown by Barker (1942). The usefulness of such choices for any but research purposes would be very limited.

The choices and rejections are likely to be more spontaneous and more in line with real likes and dislikes if they are made privately, so that individuals do not know by whom they were chosen or rejected. The information is usually written down, or, in the case of young children or illiterate older people, given orally to the investigator without being communicated to anyone else. It is treated by the investigator as confidential. This does not prevent the investigator from acting upon the information but it does minimize the possibility of unpleasant consequences to individuals. Whether the same results would be obtained when names are given orally as when they are written down is questioned by Borgatta (1951). He suggests that when the names are given orally to a teacher, the children may feel compelled to give names, whereas they might not make the same choices, and indeed might not make any choices, if they were replying to a written questionnaire.

Ideally the number of choices and rejections made by each individual should be unrestricted. Only in this way is it possible to identify positively the individuals to whom any one person is really indifferent and the individuals who are completely unchosen. In practice, the difficulty of dealing with very long lists makes it expedient to restrict the number of choices and rejections. Three of each is the most usual number. Fewer than that would present an inadequate picture of the group. More are difficult to handle. Borgatta (1951) makes the point that by asking for a particular number of choices

13

the results may be rendered unreliable. Some of the subjects may feel impelled to make more choices than they would really make, and the fact that some might make no choices at all from the group would be obscured. Not only are the choices of those who would make many restricted, but also those who would make few or no choices are forced to make the number asked for. When a class of children is given complete freedom as to the number of choices they make the resulting lists are not usually as long as might be feared. From five to seven choices is quite a usual range to find.

The question of rejections is one of extreme difficulty. Although most people are quite willing to tell an investigator which people they like in a group, they are often very unwilling to indicate their dislikes. This is sometimes from fear of repercussions, but more often from a dislike of hurting another person's feelings. Among a group of training college students to whom Cornwell (1958) administered a sociometric test, 62% voted against the inclusion of negative choices. These students said they found the making of rejections repellent and repugnant, causing bad feelings in the mind and leaving a sense of inward guilt. It was difficult to avoid prejudice, they said, and rejection was more difficult and less pleasant than choosing. At the same time they recognized that the inclusion of rejections as well as choices gave a truer picture of the group and was fairer to the great majority who, though not chosen were also not rejected. It also made it possible for something to be done to help the people who, as a result of the test, were found to be rejected.

To ask for rejections, or to press for them if they are refused, may antagonize the group and this loss of goodwill towards the investigator is bound to prejudice the results. For this reason it is very common to find that only choices, and not rejections also, are asked for. This limits the amount of information that can be extracted from the lists, since there is no indication of whether the unnamed individuals are people to whom others are indifferent or whether they are being actively rejected by others. It must be remembered that to be rejected is often more important in its effects on the individual concerned than to be chosen. It is also important to know whether there are any members of the group who make an abnormally high number of rejections.

It is important that the activities or occasions for which companions are to be chosen should be such as are within the experience of the group or which they can envisage. Equally, the request for information should be worded so as to be easily understood by the subjects. Moreno also insisted that the information asked for should relate to a real situation and that it should be acted upon. If children are asked whom they would like to sit next in class, then the class should be seated in accordance with their replies, as far as this can be done. If action were not taken on the results of a test, then Moreno said it would not be a true sociometric test. Where the situation is a hypothetical one and no action on the results is contemplated, it is usually described as 'near-sociometric'. Such tests can provide useful information about the structure of a group where the subjects are sufficiently sophisticated and co-operative to appreciate the aim. Less sophisticated or unco-operative subjects may, however, make haphazard choices if they know that no action is contemplated. Knowing that one is likely to find oneself in close proximity to the persons one names tends to reduce the number of irresponsible choices made.

Perhaps a distinction might be made between pure research investigations and the use of sociometric tests as an aid to classroom organization. Cornwell (1958) made the point that where choices have been implemented the setting has been altered and repetition of the test becomes impossible. For this reason the near sociometric test may often be more useful as a research instrument than a true test. With large groups, too, the practical difficulty of implementing choices has to be considered, and it would be a pity if the real and often important information about the group which can be gleaned from a near-sociometric test were not obtained because of this. Actual circumstances should always decide whether a true or near-sociometric test should be used on any particular occasion.

III. THE VALIDITY AND RELIABILITY OF SOCIOMETRIC TESTS

No discussion of a testing procedure can be regarded as complete without some consideration of the validity and reliability

15

of the test instruments used. Where the instrument is a sociometric test it is necessary at the outset to note an important way
in which it differs from psychometric tests. The usual psychometric test is designed to elicit a sample of behaviour from
which the possession of certain characteristics or the likelihood
of related behaviour can be inferred. The validity of the test
is a measure of the success with which it does this. The sociometric test, on the other hand, is designed to elicit the actual
behaviour being studied, and in so far as it does this it is a valid
measure of that behaviour. No reference to an outside criterion
is needed, or, indeed, possible or meaningful in this case.

The only real question which arises is whether the test
elicits a true sample of behaviour or whether the choices
expressed by the subjects are false choices. In so far as the
choices are for a real situation in which the subject will have
to associate with those he chooses, the probability is that the
choices will be true. There is a greater chance of falsification
where the situation is hypothetical or near-sociometric. Hence
Moreno's insistence on the need for a true as opposed to a
near-sociometric test when studying group structure.

In considering reliability another question arises. Is the
behaviour or quality being studied itself invariable? If it is not,
then the usual test-retest procedure for assessing reliability is
unsuitable. Where a sociometric test is repeated at a short
interval, the result may well be affected by the reliability of
the memory factor. This would tend to produce a spuriously
high reliability coefficient. Where the test is given after a long
interval, the instability of the behaviour may produce a
spuriously low reliability coefficient. Indeed, there are considerable difficulties likely to to be encountered in repeating a
sociometric test after any but a short interval. In even such a
stable group as a school class, children leave and new children
enter the class. Holidays intervene, interrupting group life.
Classes are split up on promotion to a higher grade. All these
events and many others will affect the stability of choice.

The other common method of measuring test reliability, the
split-half method, is equally unsatisfactory. For its successful
application the test must be split into two precisely equivalent
sections. Where a sociometric test is concerned the question

immediately arises as to what are equivalent samples of choice behaviour. No satisfactory answer seems possible.

In view of these considerations it seems that, as Pepinsky (1949) wrote, 'the concepts of "reliability" and "validity" as traditionally used ...... by psychologists, seem to have little direct meaning or application to the field of sociometry'. Instead the important questions seem to be concerned with means of eliciting true samples of choice behaviour and with the stability of such behaviour over periods of time, at different ages, and under varying conditions. For an exhaustive statement of the whole problem the reader is referred to Gronlund (1959).

IV. REPRESENTATION OF THE RESULTS OF A SOCIOMETRIC TEST

The best known and most striking method of representing the results of a sociometric test is by the construction of a socio-gram. Several types of sociogram have been invented, but all show in diagrammatic form the relationships between the individual members of the group. The individuals composing the group are represented by small circles, or if the group contains both sexes one is often represented by circles and the other by triangles. Initials or some other code symbols may be used to identify the individuals represented by the circles or triangles. Lines joining the circles and triangles show the choices and rejections made by the individuals. Many types of line are used. Moreno used a red line for attraction, a black one for rejection, and a dotted line for indifference. Other workers have used a continuous line for attraction and a broken line for rejection, arrow heads being used to show the direction of the feeling (Fig. 1).

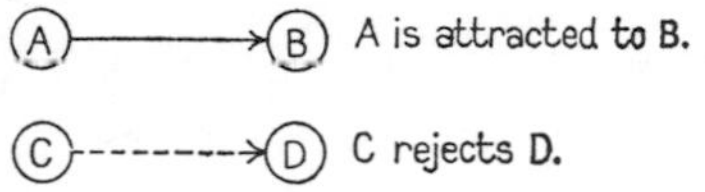

Fig. 1. Representation of choice and rejection.

Sometimes it is desirable to show the level of choice or rejection and this has been done either by using different colours for first, second and third choices, or by writing the number of the choice beside the line (Fig. 2).

Since it is frequently considered inadvisable to ask for rejections, most sociograms are in fact only choice structures. Here it is usual to assume that where no line links two individuals they are indifferent to one another, though they may

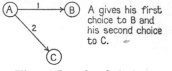

Fig. 2. Levels of choice.

actually be antagonistic. This is a point to be borne in mind if subgroups are formed as a result of testing.

Where groups are very small the drawing of a sociogram does not usually present any difficulty and the resulting diagram is easy to read and interpret. A typical example is shown in Fig. 3. The larger the group the more difficult the drawing becomes, especially if an effort is made to keep the crossing of lines to a minimum. Moreno (1953) seems to imply that where

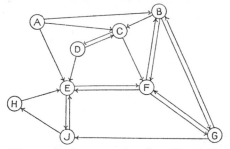

Fig. 3. Sociogram showing the choices
of working companions among a group
of students.

there are more than thirty individuals in a group it is difficult to draw a good sociogram. It is also difficult to draw a good sociogram if a large number of choices is permitted to each individual. This is a reason for restricting the choices made to three or less. If more complete information is required, an unlimited number of choices can be allowed but only the first three plotted. The sociogram can then be supplemented by reference to the original data.

18

There are a number of typical structures found in most sociograms and these are illustrated in Fig. 4. The first of these is the mutual pair, in which A is attracted to B and B is attracted to A. Then there are the chain structures, which may or may not involve mutual attractions. Closed figures, of which the triangle is the simplest, show the attractions between individuals who form cliques within the whole group. Another configuration is that where a number of individuals are attracted to one person who may or may not reciprocate their

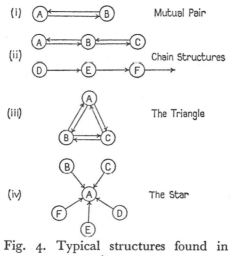

Fig. 4. Typical structures found in sociograms.

choices. This individual is usually called a 'star', from the shape of the structure surrounding him.

In most groups there are a few individuals who are not chosen by anyone else. These are often referred to as isolates, but a distinction should be made between the true isolate, who is unchosen and himself makes no choices, and the neglectee who makes choices but is not himself chosen by anyone else. A third term sometimes used is rejectee, signifying the person who is not only unchosen but is also actively rejected by other people (Fig. 5).

The main advantage of using a sociogram to show the relationships in a group lies in the ease with which it can be understood. No technical knowledge is necessary, and the information is obvious at a glance. This is not the case where information is given in the form of tables or statistical indices. Moreover all the relationships in any one group are presented at one and the same time. Added to this is the fact that sociograms nearly always arouse considerable interest in those to whom they are shown. All these points are of importance where it is required to demonstrate the structure of a group to an audience not composed of psychologists or statisticians. The sociogram is particularly useful for this purpose in both education and industry. Sanders (1943) went so far as to suggest that

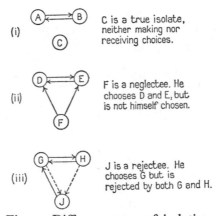

Fig. 5. Different types of isolation.

it is this type of representation of material which constitutes the real value of sociometry. He said that its appeal 'has been rather in the techniques and methods by which the data of the social sciences could be made clear to others without the verbal barrage which usually accompanies a sociological explanation of ordinary life experiences'.

The sociogram does, however, have some disadvantages. As has already been mentioned it is not easy to draw sociograms for large groups or where a large number of choices is allowed. The lay-out of the sociogram may also affect the information it conveys, and social nearness may be confused with nearness in the diagram. Suggestions for improving sociograms have been made by Northway, Proctor and Loomis, and Borgatta.

Proctor and Loomis (1951) distinguished six possible types of interpersonal relationships between two individuals i and j.

Type A, i chooses j and j chooses i.
Type B, i chooses j and j ignores i.
Type C, i chooses j and j rejects i.
Type D, i ignores j and j ignores i.
Type E, i ignores j and j rejects i.
Type F, i rejects j and j rejects i.

They suggested that these types of relationship can be arrayed along a strong-tie versus strong-aversion continuum, as shown in Fig. 6.

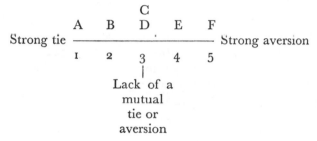

Fig. 6. Strong-tie versus strong-aversion continuum as shown by Proctor and Loomis (1951).

They pointed out that it is not entirely satisfactory to equate types C and D in this way, but they offer no alternative.

Having accepted this scheme it is theoretically possible to construct a sociogram so that the distance between any two individuals is proportional to the number in the continuum which expresses the relationship between them. They added that in order to do this for all the members of a group a multi-dimensional space may be necessary. The idea appears to be a sound one and there is something to be said for grouping together in a sociogram individuals who are linked by a choice structure and separating those who reject one another. At the same time practical difficulties may make a rigid application of this method impossible.

Borgatta (1951) described a somewhat easier method of drawing a sociogram so that the number of crossing lines is minimized and the subgroups are made apparent. He began by picking out the two, three or four persons who were most chosen and placing these in well-separated positions on a large sheet of paper. Three persons should be placed to form a triangle, four to form a square. The relationships between these people were then marked in, and their positions shifted so as to reduce the number of crossing lines. Mutual choices were shown by a double line.

Next the remainder of the group were placed on the diagram, beginning with the people who made most choices and then those who were frequently chosen. Persons who made few choices were placed next, and isolates last at the bottom of the diagram. All the time the crossing lines were kept as few as possible.

The subgroups were then identified by inspection and shifted so that they became obvious and so that persons who served as channels of communication between them could be seen. The subgroups were rearranged where necessary to cut down the number of crossing lines.

Finally the diagram was redrawn, using smaller symbols and on a smaller scale, thus making the subgroups appear as tighter units, and making the diagram more readable.

A variation of the sociogram was introduced by Northway (1940) and is called the 'target sociogram'. It consists of four concentric circles in which individuals are placed according to the number of choices they receive. The most frequently chosen are placed in the innermost ring and the least chosen in the outermost. The division of the group is made in a variety of ways. Northway originally divided the group into quarters according to the numbers of choices received (Fig. 7). Sometimes the group is divided so that those members whose choice scores differ by one or more than one standard deviation from the mean are placed in the innermost and outermost rings and the rest in the intermediate rings according as they receive more or fewer than the mean number of choices. The radii of the circles can be adjusted if desired so that the area of each division is a quarter of the area of the whole target, but this adds little to the value of the diagram.

Bronfenbrenner (1944) commented that while the target constructed in this way is satisfactory when it is only used in the study of a single group of constant membership, modifications are needed when comparisons between several groups of varying size are to be made. For such a purpose an index which has uniform significance regardless of the size of group is needed and one based on deviation from chance expectancy is suggested. For a group of a given size it is possible to calculate the number of choices which any individual might expect to receive if only chance affected the choices. It is also possible

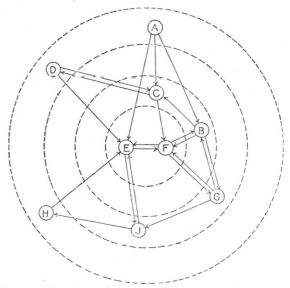

Fig. 7. Target sociogram. Compare with Fig. 3, which refers to the same group.

to calculate the chances that an individual will receive any number of choices more or less than this number. Bronfenbrenner suggested that those receiving a number of choices greater than would have been expected only twice in a hundred times by chance should be placed in the innermost circle, and that those receiving fewer than would have been expected only twice in a hundred times should be placed in the outermost circle. The middle circle would divide those receiving more than the number expected by chance from those receiving fewer than this. Tables showing these numbers for groups of

23

different sizes with varying numbers of permitted choices have been prepared (Bronfenbrenner, 1945). Patterns of choice and rejection between individuals can be shown on the target by lines in exactly the same way as on the sociogram.

A refinement of the target sociogram has been suggested by Northway and Quarrington (1946). This is used where the group can be divided according to sex, race or some other quality. The target is divided into sectors and the members of the different subgroups are placed in separate sectors. In this way the relationships between members of the subgroups can be made plain and any cleavages which exist in the total group can be brought to light.

The main advantage of the target sociogram appears to be that it enables the overchosen and underchosen members of a group to be identified at a glance. While the overchosen can be identified easily in the ordinary sociogram by the star-shaped configuration of choices surrounding them, the underchosen are not easy to identify. The target sociogram makes it easy to be sure that *all* the underchosen and overchosen individuals in a group are identified and that none have been overlooked.

Proctor and Loomis (1951) made some important points about the interpretation of sociograms. A wide variety of factors may influence the choice-rejection pattern in a group, factors such as age, previous friendships, and social status may be mentioned. Study of a sociogram may give an indication of the probable behaviour of the members of a group in a particular situation, but without some knowledge of the forces governing their choices and rejections there is little possibility of predicting their behaviour in other situations.

An alternative to the sociogram as a method of displaying sociometric data is the sociomatrix, whose construction has been described in some detail by Forsyth and Katz (1946). They begin by tabulating the choices and rejections of a group of n individuals in an $n \times n$ matrix, the names of the members being written in the same order beginning from the top left-hand corner across the top and down the left-hand margin on the matrix. Normally self-choices are not made and this is shown by placing x's or drawing a line along the main diagonal. Positive choices are shown by $+$'s and negative choices or rejections by —'s. Thus if the third individual chooses the ninth a + is put in the cell at the intersection of the third row and ninth column. In this way all the choices and rejections made in the group can be shown. A blank cell indicates indifference, neither choice nor rejection. A matrix of this type is shown in Fig. 8. The subjects were twenty-two women

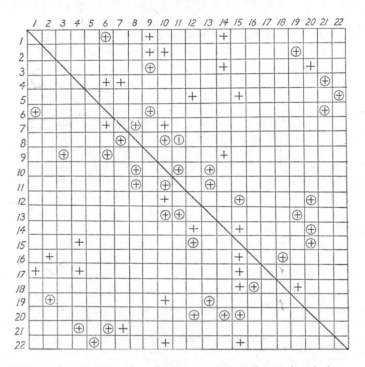

Fig. 8. Choice matrix of 22 women students (3 choices allowed). Criterion: Working together. Reciprocated choices ⊕.

students who expressed their choices of work companions. Each was allowed three choices and no rejections were made, thus only +'s appear in the cells. Mutual choices are in this case ringed.

The sociomatrix is obtained by rearranging the rows and columns of the matrix of raw data so as to make the structure of the group apparent. The first step is to select any two people between whom there is a positive mutual choice. Their rows and columns are then shifted so as to bring them to the top left-hand corner of the matrix next to one another. If any other individual is chosen by both the first two he will now be found to have a pair of +'s in the first two rows. His rows and columns are then shifted to third place, making them adjacent to those of the first two. If there is no one chosen by the first two, search is made for anyone who chooses them. If he is also chosen by one of them his rows and columns are moved to become part of their group. The process of rearrangement is continued on the principle that anyone who is chosen by at least half the members of the subgroup may be added to it. When no further persons can be found satisfying this criterion, the subgroup is considered to be complete.

A second subgroup is built up in the same way, starting with two individuals making a positive mutual choice and not included in the first subgroup. In this way a series of subgroups is built up, and a number of individuals remain who do not belong to any subgroup. Fig. 9 shows the raw data of Fig. 8 rearranged in this way.

The extent of rejection between the various subgroups can be gauged by the number of minus signs given by one group to another. The subgroups can be arranged so that those having the greatest mutual rejection are at the extremes of the principal diagonal, with other groups arranged according to degree of rejection between them. In this way blocks of minus signs are moved to the upper right-hand and lower left-hand corners of the matrix.

The unplaced individuals may or may not be satellites of subgroups. Satellites are of two kinds. Some may choose half or more than half of the members of a subgroup and be themselves rejected or ignored. It is suggested that these should be placed at the top left-hand edge of the subgroup. Others may be chosen by the members of a subgroup but not sufficiently often to be considered as belonging to it. These should be placed at the lower right-hand edge. If both these criteria apply to the same individual he should be placed in accordance with the second. Any individuals remaining when the subgroups and satellites have been placed are the genuine isolates in the group.

It is further suggested that the members of a subgroup can be rearranged so that the tighter-knit portion appears as the core or centre with subsidiary members and satellites outside.

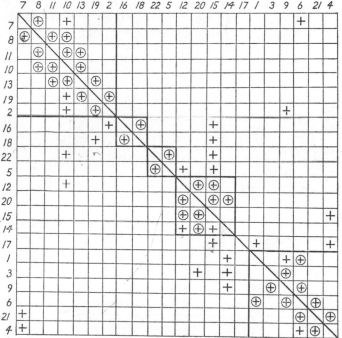

Fig. 9. Data of Fig. 8 arranged as a sociomatrix. Subgroups are outlined.

. Another method of rearranging the sociomatrix is described by Beum and Brundage (1950). They claim that it has the advantage that by using it different investigators arrive at the same results from the same data, and that the original data are preserved in the final arrangement. Subgroups, where these exist, become evident as a result of the procedure. Its authors admit, however, that the process is a long and tedious one to carry out, though it does lend itself to machine methods.

Forsyth and Katz (1946) claimed certain advantages for the sociomatrix over the sociogram. They asserted that whereas the form of the sociogram depends very much on the person drawing it, ,different investigators will produce similar or identical matrices. Groupings are made obvious by the matrix as are also the rejections between subgroups. The extent to which subgroups are well-knit is said to be an indication of their probable permanence. Stars are shown by an accumulation of +'s in their vertical columns, while rejectees are made

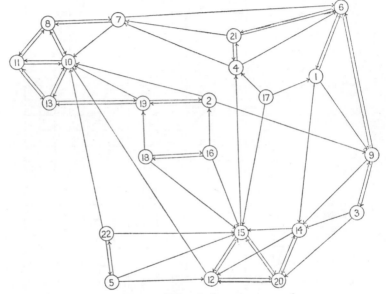

Fig. 10. Data of Fig. 8 shown as a sociogram.

obvious by the —'s. It can also be seen whether choices and rejections are general or only made by one or two subgroups. At the same time these authors admitted that the manipulation of rows and columns is a cumbersome process.

Moreno (1946) admitted that Forsyth and Katz (1946) had made a valuable contribution to sociometric practice, but he did not agree that the sociomatrix is as superior as they claim to the sociogram. He pointed out that complex structures such as the triangle and chain are more easily found from the sociogram and are, indeed, very difficult to find from the matrix

28

unless their existence is already known. The sociogram and sociomatrix should be considered as supplementary rather than opposing ways of showing sociometric data. In order that the reader may compare the two methods, the data shown in the sociomatrix in Fig. 9 are also given in the sociogram in Fig. 10.

III

THE ANALYSIS OF SOCIOMETRIC DATA

METHODS of analysis of sociometric data show an ever-increasing complexity. Starting from comparatively simple ways of measuring sociometric status, they have developed through various index methods and the consideration of variations from chance to factor analysis and the use of matrix algebra. The more recent methods are dependent on the availability of computing machines. Criswell (1946a) has pointed out that, in spite of the temptation to do so, methods of analysis commonly used in psychometrics cannot be taken over bodily and applied to sociometric data since the latter usually involve asymmetrical frequency distributions which deviate widely from normal. It is necessary both to determine the types of curve involved and to develop suitable analytical techniques. Only a few of the simpler methods of analysing sociometric data will be considered here.

I. SOCIOMETRIC STATUS

The total number of choices received by any one individual has been taken as a measure of his sociometric status in the group. These choices are, of course, made on the basis of some specified criterion, such as working together in class or playing with in the playground. When the frequency curve for the numbers of choices received by members of the group is plotted, it is unusual for the result to be a normal curve. The choices are, as a rule, distributed according to a J-curve. A few individuals, the stars, receive a large number of choices, while most members of the group receive a few choices. There are, in most groups, far more people who are under-chosen than there are over-chosen individuals. Increasing the number of choices does not alter this. The extra choices tend to go, not to the under-chosen individuals, but mainly to those already well-chosen, so that the J-curve distribution tends to become more and not less pronounced.

Thorpe (1953) found that if he included at least one negative choice or rejection when computing sociometric status scores then the distribution of scores tended to normality. This is a point worth considering. In view of the fact that the full range of choice runs from strong acceptance to strong rejection there seems little reason to expect that scores based only on the positive half of this range should be normally distributed.

This type of distribution has been compared by Moreno and Jennings (1938) with that which would have been obtained as a result of a chance distribution of choices. They asked each of twenty-six women students from each of seven groups to choose three of their number with whom she would like to sit at meals, and found that the choices were distributed according to the J-curve. They compared the results with a corresponding number of drawings from a shuffling apparatus. The curve of chance choices so obtained was approximately normal in shape.

The fact that the distribution of choices is not generally normal in shape should be borne in mind whenever the correlation of sociometric status with other measures is being studied. The theory of product-moment correlation assumes the normality of the distributions and is therefore not appropriate in such cases. Instead rank-order correlations should be used.

It is possible that the number of choices allowed may affect the sociometric ranking of a group. To test this Eng and French (1948) measured the sociometric status of thirty-two college women taking into account (1) an unlimited number of choices, (2) five choices, and (3) two choices each. They compared the results with status scores obtained by methods of paired comparisons and ranking, considering that since the method of

31

The Analysis of Sociometric Data

paired comparisons forced the ranking of each student in relation to all other students this would be the most valid method and that other methods should be judged by comparison with it. They produced the following correlation matrix but do not state what type of correlation they used.

Table 1. Correlations found by Eng and French (1948) between different measures of sociometric status

	i	ii	iii	iv	v
i. Paired comparisons		·97	·90	·73	·54
ii. Mean rank			·89	·74	·55
iii. Sum of unlimited choices				·78	·65
iv. Sum of five choices					·75
v. Sum of two choices					

It is obvious that sociometric status does vary quite considerably with different numbers of choices. The method of ranking produces a distribution not greatly different from the paired comparisons method, and as it is a much easier method it is correspondingly more useful. A sociometric test allowing unlimited choices produces a fairly satisfactory substitute for either of these methods, but the evidence here produced suggests that a test in which the number of choices is greatly restricted will not give a valid measure of status, though it will give some indication of status. If an even moderately accurate assessment is needed, less than five choices would appear to be unsatisfactory.

A question which has often been considered is whether first, second and third choices should all carry the same weight when sociometric status is being calculated. Northway (1940, 1946) has suggested giving five points for a first choice, three for a second and two for a third, but there appears to be no theoretical justification for this or any other weighting of choices, though Northway (1940) found that by using this system the scores were distributed in a form which approximated to the upper half of a normal distribution curve. Gronlund (1955) tried several weighting systems and concluded that the relative social status of his subjects was the same with weighted and unweighted scores. He obtained a median rank-difference correlation coefficient of 0·95. He also found that over a period of four months there was no difference in the relative stability of social status based on weighted and unweighted choices either with three or five choices. The stability was consistently higher with five choices than with three. He advocated basing social status scores on five unweighted choices on each sociometric criterion. Bronfenbrenner (1945) also considered unweighted scores to be a reliable index of sociometric status.

A different situation arises where choices are made on more than one criterion. Here sociometric status is often obtained by summing the choices received on all the criteria. The disadvantage of this is that the differentiation of status on the different criteria is lost. Moreno insisted that choices be made according to a definite criterion, and the assumption is that their distribution will vary from one criterion to another. The most desirable companions in a work situation may not be those who would be chosen for a leisure situation. How far choices made on different criteria agree may depend on the age and intelligence of the group. Croft and Grygier (1956) gave a sociometric test based on eight criteria to 400 boys in a London secondary modern school and found that the best indication of friendship was the general question 'Which boys do you like most?' not related to any particular situation. Gronlund (1955) found that social status scores based on a general criterion are more stable than those based on specific ones, possibly because choices on a general criterion are elicited by less modifiable characteristics of the total personality, while choices on a specific criterion depend more on constantly changing situational factors. Frankel (1946) has suggested that with pre-school children there may be a general factor of 'acceptability' which determines their status in a group. If this is so, then it may matter very little what criteria of choice are used, and the sum of choices on a variety of criteria may be the best measure of status.

Considered from another angle it is questionable whether the number of choices received is really a satisfactory indication of status in the group. Jennings (1943, 1950) has pointed out that in considering choice-status one must consider the whole setting in which it functions. It is obvious that the status of a member of a group who is chosen by four others who are themselves unchosen is very different from that of a member chosen by four who are themselves chosen by many others. Yet if sociometric status is measured by numbers of choices received these two would be rated equal in status. Katz (1953) has suggested what he describes as 'a new method of computing status, taking into account not only the number of direct "votes" received but, also, the status of each individual who chooses the first, the status of each who chooses these in turn, etc.'. Such an index of status, he claimed, 'allows for *who* chooses as well as how many choose'. The method is based on matrix algebra and is too complicated for this work. The reader who wishes to investigate it is referred to the original paper.

II. SOCIOMETRIC INDICES

A number of different types of sociometric indices have been developed. Some of these relate to the position of an individual in a group, and their main use seems to be the comparison of the relative positions of individuals who are members of different groups. Others relate to the structure of a group, and yet others are concerned with subgroups within a larger group. A number of these indices are listed by Proctor and Loomis (1951).

a. Indices relating to the position of an individual

$$\text{i's Choice status, } CS_i = \frac{\text{Number of persons choosing i}}{N - 1},$$

where N is the number of persons in the group.

$$\text{i's Rejection status, } RS_i = \frac{\text{Number of persons rejecting i}}{}.$$

$$\text{i's Positive expansiveness, } PE_i = \frac{\text{Number of choices i makes}}{N - 1}.$$

It is obvious that this last index, PE_i, can be calculated only when i is allowed an unlimited number of choices. It is described as 'a measure of i's desire to associate with other persons'.

The introduction of the divisor $(N - 1)$ calls for comment. It is used rather than N on the assumption that it is not possible for i to choose or reject himself, and that the maximum number of choices or rejections he can make is $(N - 1)$. This gives CS_1 and RS_1 a possible range from zero to $+1$. If it is only desired to compare the status of i with that of another member of the same group there is little point in introducing this divisor, since it is the same for both members. If, however, it is desired to compare the positions in their respective groups of two individuals i and j who are members of different groups, then the divisor is necessary unless the groups are of the same size. It should be noted that these indices afford no comparison between the characteristics of i and j, but only of their positions in their groups. Neither do they give any information about what their relative positions would be if they were members of the same group or of any groups except those to which they actually belong.

b. Indices relating to group structure

In addition to indices which are concerned with the status of individual members, there are a number which have been developed as measures of various properties of the group as a whole. It is sometimes desirable to know the extent to which the individuals in a group choose one another. The index of group cohesion measures this. It is given by the formula

$$C_0 = \frac{\text{Number of mutual pairs}}{\text{Possible number of mutual pairs}}.$$

The possible number of mutual pairs will depend upon the instructions as to choosing given to the group. In a group of N members whose number of choices is unrestricted, the possible number of mutual pairs is $\frac{N(N - 1)}{2}$. If the number of choices is restricted to d, this formula becomes $\frac{dN}{2}$.

A measure of the extent to which individuals are integrated into the group is given by the formula

$$I = \frac{1}{\text{Number of persons receiving no choices}}.$$

The expansiveness of a group is shown by the total number of choices made by the members of the group. In a group of N members the index of group expansiveness is given by the formula

$$E = \frac{\text{Total number of choices made by the group}}{N}.$$

These indices are all given by Proctor and Loomis (1951). They relate to choices made on one criterion and furnish a means of comparing the cohesion, integration, and expansiveness of different groups or of the same group at different times.

Work on the structure of a group as shown when multiple criteria of choice are allowed has been done by Criswell (1946b). She pointed out that where an individual A makes an unreciprocated choice of B under criterion 1, and B makes an unreciprocated choice of A under criterion 2, a closer relationship between A and B exists than might be suggested by their unreciprocated choices, and that such cross-relationships should be taken into account in considering the coherence of the group.

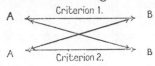

Thus if A and B make mutual choices under two criteria, they also form two cross-pairs. In general, if there are c criteria and cross-relationships are employed, then a choice is counted not once but c times, and if d choices are allowed on each of c criteria, then an individual makes cd choices per criterion and $c^2 d$ choices in all.

The chance number of reciprocated choices was obtained by Moreno and Jennings (1945) by the formula $p = \dfrac{d}{N-1}$.

The chance number of unreciprocated choices is $q = 1 - p$. Criswell (1946b) gave the number of reciprocated choices to be expected by chance where cross-relationships are allowed as

$$R_{cc} = c^2 N(N-1)p^2,$$

and the corresponding number of unreciprocated choices as

$$U_{cc} = c^2 N(N-1)pq.$$

From this it follows that the ratio of reciprocated to unreciprocated choices is

$$\frac{R_{cc}}{U_{cc}} = \frac{p}{q}.$$

If the number of reciprocated choices obtained experimentally is R and the corresponding number of unreciprocated choices is U, all cross-relationships being counted,

$$I_{cc} = \frac{Rq}{Up}.$$

This relates the experimentally determined ratio of reciprocated to unreciprocated choices to the chance ratio. The formulae apply only when d, the number of choices permitted, is constant for all criteria and from subject to subject.

c. Indices of subgroup structure

Measures of the extent to which any group prefers itself to any other group have been developed by Criswell (1943, 1944). These depend on the numbers of ingroup and outgroup choices made. Numbers of choices actually made are compared with the numbers which would be expected if chance and not preference determined the number of intergroup choices.

Suppose a group of N persons contains a subgroup of N_1 persons. The probability that a member of group 1 will choose a person in his own group is $\frac{N_1 - 1}{N - 1}$, and the probability that he will choose a person outside group 1 is $\frac{N - N_1}{N - 1}$. If group 1 makes a total of t_1 choices, then

$$\text{Number of expected ingroup choices} = \frac{t_1 (N_1 - 1)}{N - 1},$$

$$\text{Number of expected outgroup choices} = \frac{t_1 (N - N_1)}{N - 1},$$

$$\text{Chance ratio of ingroup to outgroup choice} = \frac{N_1 - 1}{N - N_1}.$$

The observed ratio of ingroup to outgroup choices can be obtained by noting the numbers of ingroup and outgroup choices actually made by the members of group 1. Suppose these are X_1 and Y_1 respectively, where $X_1 + Y_1 = t$. Then the index of ingroup preference is given by

$$IP = \frac{X_1}{Y_1} \Big/ \frac{N_1 - 1}{N - N_1} = \frac{X_1(N - N_1)}{Y_1(N_1 - 1)}$$

37

If IP>1, then the members of the group prefer themselves to others. If IP<1, then they prefer outgroup members to themselves.

If t=total number of choices made by the whole group of N persons,

and X=total number of choices received by group 1,

then the index of ingroup cleavage is given by

$$IC = \frac{X_1}{t_1} \Big/ \frac{X}{t} = \frac{X_1 t}{X t_1}$$

III. ANALYSIS OF THE SOCIOMATRIX

Matrix algebra has been used by some workers to assist in the analysis of sociometric data. Festinger (1949) has shown how it can be used to identify the patterns of connections among the members of a group.

Suppose C is the choice matrix of a group of individuals, in which a figure 1 in the cell at the intersection of row 3 and column 5 means that person 3 has chosen person 5. Where no choice has been made this is shown by a zero in the corresponding cell. Since it is usually assumed that an individual cannot choose himself, all the diagonal cells will contain zeros. If now the matrix C is squared, the resulting matrix will show the number of two-step chains connecting the individual members. If, for example, person 3 chooses person 5, who in turn chooses person 8, a figure 1 will appear in the cell at the intersection of row 3 and column 8. If a figure 2 appears in the cell at the intersection of row 3 and column 7, it means that person 3 chooses two people who in turn choose person 7. Numbers in the diagonal cells of the squared matrix indicate the numbers of mutual choices in which the individual persons are involved.

By an extension of the principle, the cube of matrix C gives the number of three-step chains between the individuals, and the matrix raised to the power *n* gives the number of *n*-step chains between them.

This applies to matrices showing both reciprocated and unreciprocated choices. If only the matrix of reciprocated choices is used, an inspection of the cubed matrix can lead to the identification of cliques within the group. A clique is here defined as a group of two or more individuals, all of whom choose each other mutually.

When the matrix of choices is cubed, numbers will appear in the diagonal cells if, and only if, a clique or cliques exist in the group. For a clique of n members, the numbers appearing in their diagonal cells will be $(n - 1)(n - 2)$. For example, if there is a clique of three members their diagonal cells will contain the number $2 \times 1 = 2$. The members of a clique of four members will have in their diagonal cells the number $3 \times 2 = 6$. The identification of the other members of a clique is aided by the knowledge that their cell values in the cubed matrix row of the first member must be greater than $[(n - 1)(n - 2) + 1]$. If $n = 3$, this expression is equal to three. If $n = 4$, it equals 7. A more detailed account of the use of this method has been given by Chabot (1950).

Where two or more sociometric tests are applied to the same group of people it is sometimes important to know to what extent the results agree with one another. It may be that different criteria have been used for the tests, or it may be that the same criterion has been used on different occasions and it is desired to find out whether the relationships in the group have changed in the interval between the tests. Obvious changes may be found by inspection of the sociograms or sociomatrices. This method, while it can yield useful results, does not give a measure of conformity. Such a measure has been described by Katz and Powell (1953). It is called an index of conformity. While its existence should be known, its calculation is a somewhat complicated procedure beyond the scope of an introductory work such as this. The reader who wishes to know more about it should refer to the original paper for a detailed account of this index.

IV

POPULARITY AND ISOLATION

THE value of sociometric techniques in the study of classroom relationships is obvious. It is possible by their use to discover both the relative social status of the children and the networks of relationships by which they are linked together, and during the last decade teachers have made increasing use of sociometric tests for these purposes. It is eminently desirable that they should continue to do so, but a word of warning is necessary. It is not safe to assume that the children who are most often chosen and thus have the highest sociometric status are in fact the most influential members of the class. A distinction must be made between popularity and leadership, and in order to do this both the sociometric status of the child and its position in the network must be considered.

In many studies which have appeared this distinction has not been made clear. It is comparatively simple to measure the sociometric status of children, but it is much less easy to assess their leadership status, and this probably accounts for the uncritical assumption by some workers that the two are identical. If leadership is to be studied then the sociometric test must deal with a situation in which leadership has to be exercised. It is not enough to assume that the children chosen most often as classroom neighbours are also those who are accepted as leaders of classroom life. They are much more likely to be the children whose social or other gifts make them pleasant companions.

40

Since to be socially acceptable is a desirable characteristic it is important for teachers to understand the factors that make children acceptable to one another. Only with this knowledge can they set about the social training of their children. For most people to be accepted as a social companion is more important than to be accepted as a leader, and there is no stigma attaching to studies of popularity. Indeed the reverse is the case, as long as they are not offered as studies of leadership.

A question which must arise is whether there is any general factor of social acceptability or whether people are acceptable or not according to the situation they are in and the companions of the moment. Northway (1943) reported a study by Budden dealing with the consistency of social acceptability of pre-school children. It was found that thirty-six children in a nursery school were well-differentiated in social acceptability to one another, and that there was considerable consistency of acceptability for different activities. This was particularly the case with the most and least acceptable children. The same article contains a report of a research by Gregory in which it was obvious that among fourteen four-year-olds observed preference and not chance factors governed the choice of companions. This conclusion was also supported by Frankel (1946), and Bonney (1943b) obtained similar results when working with children of junior school age. Social acceptance appeared to be almost as constant year by year as such things as intelligence and academic achievement. Changes in friendships might occur, but the general level of acceptability of the children relative to one another remained much the same. The conclusion drawn is that it is difficult to change the impression a child makes upon his own group, and that the child who is maladjusted in one group is likely to be so in another also.

Morgan (1951) carried out a study of attractions and repulsions in a class of thirty-one children entering a London grammar school. During their first year in the school they were asked, at approximately six-week intervals, to choose the companions with whom they would like to sit in the classroom. The pattern of group relationships was found to be remarkably stable, and such changes as occurred were changes of emphasis

D   41

rather than of kind. The relative popularity of the children remained much the same, but it was discovered that most of them were rejected at some time during the year. For some of them this happened only rarely, for others the rejection was more or less continuous. Kerstetter (1946) carried out a rather similar study with American children of about the same age. Here the testing was carried on over a period of three years and the results showed that the boys' scores remained more nearly constant than those of the girls. Wertheimer (1957) correlated sociometric status scores of a group of adolescents made at three testings between March 1953 and November 1954 and obtained coefficients between 0·56 and 0·72, all significant at the 1% level for both boys and girls. Since product-moment correlations were used, one would have to know whether the scores were normally distributed or not before accepting this result at its face value.

The suggestion that the social climate of the classroom may have some effect on the constancy of the sociometric status of the pupils was made by Taylor (1952). He tested over a thousand eighth-grade boys and girls over a period, and found that social acceptance scores were as constant as intelligence quotients are reputed to be, but that they were less constant in the more progressive classrooms. This, he considers, is the result of the ways in which more progressive teachers deal with the social problems of their pupils. Support for this view is found in an observation by Bonney (1955) that among college students there was a much stronger tendency for sociometrically high students to remain high than for sociometrically low students to remain low. The most marked long-term changes were made by students who were originally low but whose adjustment to the group improved, either with or without outside help, over a period of time.

A great deal of research has been done on the factors which make people acceptable to one another. It is possible that these factors are not the same at all ages, but if the reports already mentioned are correct, it seems likely that the people who are acceptable at one age will remain so as they get older. In the study by Budden already mentioned it was suggested that among pre-school children maturity may contribute to acceptability. At this age differences of a few months in age may correspond to quite marked differences in social skills, and these skills make for acceptability. Certainly Budden found that the older children in her nursery school group had a higher sociometric status than the younger ones. Frankel (1946), too, seemed to think that personality development rather than more objective factors may make for acceptability.

Observations among older children and students suggest that the connection between maturity and sociometric status is doubtful. Taylor (1952) found that younger children were more acceptable to their classmates than older children. On the other hand, Thorpe (1953) found that in a large sample of London children, nearly all in secondary modern schools and divided between thirty-four classes, there was a tendency for the older children to be more popular than the younger ones. Popularity in this case was judged on four sociometric criteria: sitting by in class, playing with at break, taking home to tea and liking least in the class. Gustad (1952), reviewing the literature on the subject, concluded that among college students age and maturity seemed associated with wider social activities.

Age and maturity are not always synonymous among children and some studies using other criteria of maturity than age have been reported. Heber (1956) used height as a criterion of physical maturity among junior school children, but he himself admitted that it might not be a good one. He found no difference in sociometric status between the groups he classed as of high, average and low maturity. It is possible that maturity may be more closely associated with leadership than with popularity, and this proposition will be considered in a later chapter.

The importance of language development in the social relationships of young children is brought out by Rosenthal (1957). The groups he studied were small, but his results deserve serious consideration. Out of 358 children in eleven second-grade classes in six schools he chose two groups each of ten boys and ten girls, matched for age and intelligence quotients, one of high and the other of low sociometric status. Samples of their spoken language were evaluated and compared

43

in terms of its structure, method and communicative value, and the results showed that although the two groups used much the same number of words, the more popular children used language of a superior quality and social usefulness. They were differentiated from children of low sociometric status in terms of language which was more active, variable and communicative to another individual. It seems likely that the capacity to communicate with others is an important factor in the determination of a child's popularity, but Taylor (1952) suggested that it may be more important in some contexts than others. He found that in classrooms where traditional methods of instruction were used, what he calls 'non-verbal' children were at less of a disadvantage socially than in more progressive classrooms. In the more progressive settings children move about more freely and mix and talk together more than they do where traditional methods are used, and here their capacity to communicate in speech may have a greater effect on their social standing.

A more obvious basis of social attractiveness is personal appearance. Our first assessments of people we meet are formed as a result of the impression made on us by their appearance. Beauty or ugliness, neatness in dress, body build, ways of moving, facial expression, are all noted and help to build up our picture of the person and to determine the effect he or she produces on us. Some people we like on sight, others repel us, and many arouse little or no feeling. Barker (1942) found that when a sociometric test was given to a group of twelve university students who were complete strangers to one another, they expressed preferences for seat mates among the members of the group, and the resulting sociogram showed the presence among them of stars, isolates and reciprocal pairs. Good looks appeared to be the characteristic most highly related to desirability in this case. Young and Cooper (1944) found that among children in grades five to eight the most striking difference between the highest and lowest eighth on popularity was in facial attractiveness, and Kuhlen and Lee (1943) obtained a similar result with slightly older boys and girls. There can be little doubt that an attractive appearance is a great aid at least to initial popularity. Whether it will outweigh other disadvantages after longer acquaintance is open to question, and may depend on the standards of the particular group.

In view of the large number of intelligence tests available and the ease with which they can be administered to school classes, it is not surprising to find that sociometric status has frequently been considered in relation to intelligence. Some workers have reported a tendency for these two variables to be positively correlated, but in most cases the correlation has been low. Heber (1956) suggested that this result may have been obtained because the methods of investigation used postulated a rectilinear relationship between intelligence and sociometric status. If this is not the case, then correlational techniques may not detect the relationship. If the relationship is curvilinear then a comparison of upper and lower thirds might be better suited to detecting it. An observation by Bonney (1943a) that when a whole class was considered the correlation between social acceptance and intelligence scores was low, but that upper fourths were superior to lower fourths on both, seems to support this view.

Heber (1956) himself reported a study in which he compared the intelligence and social status of junior school children. He divided the group into three according to intelligence, and found that the children of high intelligence were, on the average, markedly higher in sociometric status than the children of low intelligence. He also found children of low intelligence were farther below average in sociometric status than those of high intelligence were above. He suggests that intelligence is important only up to a point in determining sociometric status, and that the relationship is likely to be exponential rather than rectilinear. This is supported by Grossman and Wrighter (1948) who found that while children of below normal intelligence were of inferior sociometric status, the status of children of average intelligence did not differ significantly from that of children whose intelligence was superior to average. Provided a child's intelligence is not markedly below normal, it seems to have little effect on his popularity with other children.

The influence of academic achievement on popularity seems to be similar to that of intelligence. Bonney (1955) and Smith (1945) found that students who ranked high sociometrically

45

and were socially active tended to have a higher level of achievement than those who ranked low. Grossman and Wrighter (1948) found that among sixth-grade pupils a reading achievement which was below average was associated with low sociometric status, but that beyond that achievement did not appear to affect status. As in the case of intelligence, it seems likely that the relationship between sociometric status and achievement in school subjects is exponential rather than linear.

The extent to which socio-economic status influences a child's popularity among his fellows has been the subject of a number of investigations. Smith (1945) noted that among older adolescents those taking part in extra-curricular activities tended to be of higher socio-economic status, but this is not direct evidence that they were also more popular than the average. Gustad (1952), too, found a general tendency for home factors such as the level of socialization and socio-economic level to affect social participation. Grossman and Wrighter (1948) considered that the effect of socio-economic status was limited, and that as long as a child was not from a home of below lower middle class it made little difference to his social acceptability at school. Very low family social status appeared to be a disadvantage, but apart from that children took little notice of the family level of their fellows. Becker and Loomis (1948) considered that personal characteristics rather than family background were the determiners of a child's popularity at school, and they found that this was very markedly true in the cases of children who were rejected or neglected by others.

Bonney (1943a) expressed the view that a child is accepted by his fellows because of what he does rather than of what he does not do, and that strong positive personality traits are more important than negative virtues. A friendly attitude, too, is important in winning friends. Kuhlen and Lee (1943) supported this view, and said that in a group of 700 boys and girls in grades six, nine and twelve, the most acceptable individuals were described as being cheerful and happy, enthusiastic, friendly, enjoying jokes, and initiating games and other activities. The relationship between these traits and popularity became apparent with development into adolescence, when the active, socially aggressive extraverts held the field. Young and Cooper (1944) also recorded that the more extraverted children were more popular than others, and that popularity was linked with a stronger feeling of belonging to the group, the expression of more acceptable social standards, and superior school relations. It would be easy to multiply examples, but the picture of the type of personality usually found to be most acceptable in the classroom emerges clearly from the inquiries already quoted.

One other quality associated with popularity deserves mention. This is sensitivity. Northway and Wigdor (1947) found that boys and girls who were highly acceptable socially showed greater sensitivity than those less highly accepted in sensing the feelings of others, and displayed a conscious striving for the approval of others. Loban (1953) also reported that the most sensitive adolescents in a group of over 400 were clearly more popular with their peers than were the least sensitive adolescents, and that the difference in popularity between the most and least sensitive groups was significant at the 1% level. This seems to suggest that the most popular classroom personality is the happy, friendly extravert who understands and considers the feelings of others.

An important aspect of social acceptability is its relationship to maladjustment and delinquency. That acceptance by others is a strong factor making for a good personal adjustment was shown by Potashin (1946). In a study of children's friendships it was found that a child who had a close personal friend was usually accepted by others, but that the child who had no such close friend, although not rejected, was not sought as a companion. As a result, his own choices tended to be unreal and directed to the 'stars' of the group. Other workers have noted this tendency of the isolate to choose the star. It may be a defence mechanism in that no one will expect an impossible choice to be reciprocated, whereas the lack of reciprocation of a more natural choice might draw adverse notice.

It is evident from studies by Grossman and Wrighter (1948), McClelland and Ratliff (1947) and Kuhlen and Bretsch (1947) that children who are not well-accepted by their class-

47

mates often have more social problems than most and show more nervous symptoms than the average. These studies bring out the importance of social skills to adolescents, and Kuhlen and Collister (1952) go so far as to suggest that social maladjustment may be to some so important that it results in their actually leaving school earlier than their better-adjusted contemporaries. Gustad (1952) has remarked that the general picture presented by the literature shows that adolescents who participate in social activities tend to show less maladjustment than those who do not.

As opposed to these results, Thorpe (1953), whose sample of London school children was made up of classes each of which contained one child who attended a child guidance clinic, found that neuroticism was not of paramount importance in differentiating popular from unpopular pupils. When intelligence was partialled out the importance of neuroticism was increased, but its influence was still not high. Hallworth (1952) found no evidence that grammar-school children of average sociometric status were less neurotic than those of high or low status, but this does not agree with the findings of Northway and Wigdor (1947). They found that the Rorschach Inkblot Test responses of both the high and low status groups differed from normal more than did the responses of the intermediate group. The unaccepted group appeared to be more severely disturbed than either of the others.

Croft and Grygier (1956) investigated social relationships among boys in a London secondary modern school where roughly 10% of the pupils were classed as delinquents or truants. Social status was based on the results of a sociometric test involving eight criteria and asking for both preferences and rejections. It was found that in general both truants and delinquents had lower sociometric status than other boys. The truants were more socially maladjusted than the delinquents and had few friends. The delinquents tended to have many enemies, and the suggestion is made that delinquency may sometimes be a defence against extreme isolation. It was found that while popularity was fairly evenly distributed, dislike seemed to be concentrated on a few boys, and that increasing the size of the group increased the number of their enemies without increasing the number of their friends. This supports from the negative side the view that there is a general factor of social acceptability, and indicates the wisdom of placing unpopular boys in small groups wherever possible, so as to decrease the amount of dislike with which they have to contend.

One way in which the classroom group can be manipulated to help children who are becoming maladjusted has been described by Kerstetter (1940). When a series of sociometric tests based on the criterion of sitting together was administered to a group of fifth-grade children over a period of ten months, it was found that one subgroup of five boys was badly adjusted to the group as a whole. There was an increasing tendency for them to concentrate all their choices within their subgroup and to be at first unchosen and later rejected by the other children. The boys all lived and played in the same area and they began to develop delinquent tendencies outside the school. The results of the sociometric tests made their teacher aware of the situation, and when the opportunity arose to rearrange the seating of the class the subgroup was split up, two of them being put in one work group and three in another. As a result, new friendships were formed and the boys were no longer cut off from the rest. This improvement was reflected outside school, where their delinquent activities ceased and they began to take part in constructive community activities instead.

It will be obvious by now that popularity seems to be as much a matter of chance as anything else. Perhaps it is comforting to reflect that for most people it is more important to have a few friends than to be a popular idol, and friendship is not a matter of the qualities of one individual, but of a mutual relationship between two people or among the members of a group. For this reason, studies such as that of Potashin (1946) may well be of more value to teachers and others who are concerned with the adjustment of children to one another, than studies of the concomitants of popularity. Potashin, who defined friends as pairs of children in which each gave the other his highest choice on a sociometric test, studied such pairs as units. The results showed that friends tended to resemble one another slightly, and that sociological factors were more important than physical ones in determining friendships. Friends were found

49

to be at ease together in a discussion situation, to talk freely and for some length of time, and to require little adult prompting. Pairs of children in which one chose the other but did not have his choice reciprocated were much less at ease, and the poorly accepted child frequently caused tension by trying to impress his partner, either by a too ready agreement or by showing off.

In a survey of literature on friendship among children, Frankel and Potashin (1944) noted that early researches stressed the similarities and differences between friends. In the main, more similarities than differences are reported. Smith (1944) found that adolescents selected as friends others in their group whom they resembled in one or more characteristics, which included sex, church preference and various factors related to their homes and parents. Jenkins (1931) found that children tended to choose friends within a year of their own age and of similar intelligence level and socio-economic status. Sower (1948), on the other hand, found no significant relationship between the occupations of the fathers of choosers and chosen.

Precker (1952) made the suggestion that in a group of students and staff in a small progressive college, there was a tendency for friendship choices to go to others whose values resembled their own, and that this was most marked when reciprocal choices were made. Smith (1944) noted religious affiliation as a factor in friendship choices, but this was not strongly supported by the findings of Evans and Wilson (1949). In a group of 148 women students, minority groups of Jewish, Roman Catholic and Christian Science students gave the greater number of their choices outside their own religious groups, but 82% of the choices of the whole group went to members of their own classes. Most chose as friends students whose rooms were on the same floor of the hall of residence as their own. Intellectual interest and proximity evidently outweighed common religious convictions in this case.

Northway and Detweiler (1955) found that a group of children, who rated themselves, their friends, and others to whom they were indifferent on ten good qualities, tended to perceive their friends as possessing desirable qualities to a higher degree than they did themselves. Those to whom they were indifferent were perceived as possessing these good qualities to a lesser degree than they did themselves. Friendship, here, seemed to have the element of admiration in it, and this may be a factor in friendship formation.

Studies of the concomitants of friendship usually give no indication of its origin, and do not show how the relationship actually works. Where similarities and differences between friends are observed, there is always the question as to whether they are a reason for the growth of the friendship or whether they are a result of the association. Are friends people who resemble one another and who join forces because of this, or does the friendship they feel for one another cause them, consciously or otherwise, to change their original behaviour so that eventually they become like one another? Possibly the answer is that both these are true. Some characteristics, like appearance and intelligence, are less changeable than others, but interests and value systems can be changed relatively easily when there is an adequate motive for the change. Friendship may provide such a motive.

Another basis for friendship was suggested by Shukla (1951), who saw it as satisfying the growing needs of children for affection and love, security and identification, and as an aid in coping with growing self-consciousness. Friends, he suggests, are selected according to the degree to which they help to satisfy these needs. His subjects were 252 pupils in a mixed secondary modern school near London, whose ages were roughly between 12 and 15 years and whose mental ages ranged from 7 years 9 months to 15 years 10 months. The majority came from average middle-class families in a small town and the surrounding villages. These boys and girls tended to choose as their friends others from the same school and the families of mutual friends were usually well acquainted. Friends were often alike mentally and physically, with similar tastes and temperaments, likes and dislikes, and the basis of many friendships appeared to be mutual understanding and also an appreciation of dissimilarities.

Those children who are ignored or rejected by others constitute one of the greatest problems a teacher has to deal

51

with in the classroom. Some of them will wish to be accepted by other children, some of them will not care. In either case they are maladjusted in the classroom group, and there is at least a possibility that they will be maladjusted in other groups as well. Most of them need help, and this can only be given effectively if the cause of their isolation is understood.

One of the most important studies of isolation was made by Northway (1944). Among children in grades five and six she found three different types of isolate, whom she classified as recessive, socially uninterested, and socially ineffective. The recessives were listless, lacking in vitality and physically below par. Their intelligence was low and their achievement was poor, they were generally careless about their appearance, possessions and work, and they showed little interest in the world around them.

The socially uninterested children were superficially similar to the recessives in that they were quiet and retiring and made no effort socially. In contrast to the recessives they took more care of their persons and possessions and had interests and hobbies, though these tended to be personal rather than social. Some of them were quiet and uninterested in other children, others were shy and uncomfortable in society, or bored and critical. In some cases these children enjoyed watching rather than joining in social activities.

The socially ineffective children did want to join in, but did not know how to do so. They were often noisy and rebellious, boastful and arrogant, sometimes delinquent and usually a nuisance in class. They had plenty of vitality and made ineffective and naïve attempts to overcome their insecurity and isolation.

Children may become isolates for a variety of reasons. Some children deliberately withdraw from the society of others, neither wanting nor seeking attention. Gronlund (1959) described what he called the 'self-sufficient' isolate, who has his own interests and pursues them happily by himself. These children often welcome interest in their activities and are willing to talk about them and show them off to others, but they do not need a great deal of companionship. Their accomplishments gain them enough prestige and a few like-minded friends provide enough social activity. Such children are not a serious problem.

Some children who withdraw deliberately may do so because they fear rejection or do not know how to mix with others. These may be emotionally disturbed and need specialist attention, or they may be merely lacking in social skills and in need of help in acquiring them and building up their self-confidence. This is work for the class teacher. Kuhlen and Bretsch (1947) found that socially unaccepted adolescents were often concerned about their lack of social skill and wanted help in improving. The stress caused by this can sometimes result in drastic withdrawal, to the extent of leaving school prematurely, as was found by Kuhlen and Collister (1952).

Active rejection of some children by the majority is a different problem. Not infrequently the rejectee differs in some way from the rest of the group, and this is true not only among children but also, as was shown by Kidd (1951), among college students. The difference may be of intelligence, race, creed, social class or age, or it may be of the nature of physical deformity. In some of these cases social isolation may not be obvious to the teacher. Bonney (1943b) cited instances where a crippled girl and a boy of another race were always treated by the other children with great kindness and sympathy, and it was only when a sociometric test asking for names of preferred companions was given that it became apparent that neither of these children was really chosen by any of the others. Bonney (1943a) also showed how strict control by the teacher may mask differences in status among the children. Strict control, by giving the children less chance of self-assertion, may prevent them from displaying their capabilities and weaknesses, and may thus hamper their assessment of one another as companions. In a teacher-dominated classroom a class may appear to lack both leaders and isolates.

Personality defects may also be a cause of isolation in children. In a classic study of leadership and isolation Jennings (1943 and 1950) found that isolates tended to be 'self-bound' and unable to bridge the gap between themselves and others. Children of whom this is true need to be given training in making contact with other people. As Partridge (1943) remarked, 'it is almost certain that the only way an individual can learn to become an acceptable group member is by practice at it over a period of time'. At the same time, merely placing isolated children in existing groups is not always the best way to help them. Bonney (1943a) has made the point that this is not likely to result in the child's being better accepted unless he has a definite contribution to make to the activities of the group. It is therefore of the first importance that children who are isolated should only be placed in groups in which they have a chance of making a successful adjustment. To group together a number of isolates is to court disaster. The very qualities which make them unacceptable to other people are likely also to make them unacceptable to one another. If this were not the case they would have been more likely to have been the members of a clique, cut off from the rest of the class, rather than isolates.

The attitude of the teacher may in some cases be a factor leading to rejection and isolation. Croft and Grygier (1956) found that, in a secondary modern school, boys whom the teachers regarded as being badly behaved tended to be rejected by the rest. An amusing qualification of this statement was that this tendency was less marked in the more backward classes. It would appear that backward boys were less ready or able to accept the values of the school than their more intelligent companions. It is at least possible that this may not mean that the values of the school were being actively rejected, so much as that they were not being perceived by the less able boys.

It is, of course, not necessarily true that children who are not accepted at school are isolated in other groups. Pearce (1958) reported that boys who were of low sociometric status in the C-forms of a grammar school were often very active in evening youth clubs and in street corner society. On the other hand Croft and Grygier (1956) found that when a boys' club was formed near a secondary modern school, maladjusted as well as well-adjusted boys from the school joined it, but that the maladjusted ones soon left. This may have been due to the fact that they met at the club the same boys whom they met at school, and so were equally maladjusted to the group both in club and school. There is, however, a real possibility that the child who is maladjusted in one group will be maladjusted in others, and that is why it is so important that the isolates should be identified and helped.

Northway (1944) added an important caveat when she spoke of the danger of assuming that high social acceptance is always desirable. People differ in the extent to which they can make social contacts, some being able easily to maintain relations with many friends, others being happiest with a few companions. That students differ considerably in this way was shown by Evans (1952a). In helping a child to a good social adjustment it is necessary to consider what type will be best for the individual. Often a small group of congenial friends is more satisfying than wider popularity.

Bonncy (1943b) has pointed out that no one should assume that because he has serious personality difficulties he will not be well-accepted by others. The important thing is that the child should be helped to acquire at least one close personal friend who prefers his company to that of others. Bonney wrote, 'unless a person is a preferred companion of at least a few other people, he cannot have a close friend, he (or she) will not be selected as a marriage partner, and he will probably feel socially insecure all his life — even though nobody dislikes him or ever does anything against him'. Some children will be easy to help to a good social adjustment, others will be more difficult, but there can be no doubt that it is of the first importance that the task should be realized and undertaken.

V

LEADERSHIP

AT the other end of the scale from the isolates are the leaders of the group. The term leader is used in so many different ways that it seems necessary to begin by listing some of them. For example, we talk about leaders in art or science or commerce when we mean people who are successful in these fields, whose attainments are high, and who have influenced the development of thought and practice in their own spheres. We talk about leaders in public life when we mean people who hold high office. Often these people have to make decisions and speak for others. They have been invested with authority which may have been inherited or have been conferred on them by popular vote or acclaim. Again, we may use the term leader of the member of a group who, when a situation requiring action arises, takes over the direction of other members and guides either what they do or what they think.

In any case, a leader is a person who influences other people, but this is not a sufficient definition, since wherever two or more people are in contact any one of them is likely to influence the rest, but all are not leaders. A leader is a member of a group who influences others more than they influence him, who guides the group towards attaining its goals, and who may, in fact, determine what those goals shall be.

It is necessary at this stage to distinguish two types of influence over other people. One may be called leadership and the other headship. The difference is that the influence of a leader is

voluntarily accepted, while headship is charactèrized by
domination from without. Headship is maintained by forces
other than spontaneous acceptance by the group. There is
little shared interest between group and head in the choice of
goals and the manner of their pursuit, and there is usually a
wide social gap between the head and the group. The head is
not, in fact, usually seen by the group as 'one of themselves'.
The leader, on the other hand, is seen as one of the group and
his authority derives from their spontaneous reaction to him.
They and he have the same goals and they act together to
achieve them.

Relationships of both these types are found in school. The
teacher, in relation to the class, usually exercises headship
rather than leadership, since his authority does not originally
derive from the class. Within the class there are nearly always
children who are accepted by others as leaders.

Perhaps it may be wise to point out that there is no contrast
of good and bad between leadership and headship. The situation, the people, and the way in which power is exercised have
all to be taken into account in making any moral judgment.
Headship may be tyranny or it may be benevolent and constructive. Leadership may be wise or foolish.

Most members of a group actively desire that someone shall
direct their activities, and where the person whom they expect
to act as leader refuses to take up his role they are likely to
become uneasy and unhappy, and the group may be thoroughly
demoralized if the situation persists for any length of time.
Descriptions of groups of adults who were brought together to
study their own behaviour have been given by Trist and Sofer
(1959). Experts who were present refused to assume leadership
and the members attempted to deal with their own discomfort
in a variety of ways, by denying its existence, by silence, by
ignoring the expert, by amusement or scepticism, or by taking
refuge in other topics. Considerable stress was experienced by
the members of these groups. That children also are unhappy
in a group where leadership is lacking seems clear from a
consideration of the 'laissez-faire' groups in Lippitt and White's
(1943) experiment. Ten-year-old boys, in the care of an adult
who made no attempt to control or direct their activities, did

E   57

little constructive work and showed little co-operative behaviour. When opportunity occurred, a leader from among the boys took charge of the group, and this is what frequently happens in such situations. The chaos of an unstructured group, lacking leaders, where the members have no definite role or status relationships to one another, seems to be more than most human beings can endure.

A very large number of studies of leadership have been reported, dealing both with adult and children's groups. Many of the studies of adult leadership were carried out in the armed forces. Stogdill (1948) has distinguished five methods used in these studies.

i.   Observation of behaviour in group situations.

ii.   Choice of associates.

iii.   Nomination or rating by qualified observers.

iv.   Selection (and rating or testing) of persons occupying leadership positions.

v.   Analysis of biographical and case history data.

As Bogardus (1934) pointed out, leadership is a group phenomenon, and the leader implies the follower. No one can be a leader in isolation and leadership always arises in social situations. Jennings (1937) found several different types of leadership among a large group of adolescent girls, and it seems likely that the same types will be found in many school classes. The first type were those who were only occasionally leaders, and that only when a situation arose in which they could use some particular talent. Except on these occasions they were undistinguished members of the group. The second type were girls whose sphere of influence was limited. They were chosen as leaders by only a few other group members, and by those who were isolated or of little influence themselves. The third type were those who had a broad sphere of influence which lasted only for a short time. None of these three types would exert strong or lasting influence on the group as a whole.

The remaining types were more important. One consisted of persons whose influence gradually increased until it affected

58

and was accepted by the majority of the group. Their influence was both widespread and lasting. The other type was what Jennings called the 'aristo-tele' leader, the person who had few direct contacts but who was accepted by other members who were themselves in stable leadership positions. The influence of the 'aristo-tele' leader was thus spread through the group because of the contacts of these more generally accepted leaders.

Wolman (1958) classified leaders according to their personal aims. An instrumental leader, he said, uses the resources of his followers for his own benefit. One who is willing to serve his followers but hopes to be served by them too is called a mutual acceptance leader. The third type is the vectorial leader, who does not present a bill for his services and whose only endeavour is to make other people happy. In Wolman's opinion, all great spiritual leaders have been vectorial leaders.

Cattell and Stice (1954) identified four types of leader among small groups of young men who were observed while carrying out a variety of tasks. The first type were the persistent momentary problem solvers, who made frequent brief acts of leadership. These would appear to correspond to Jennings's first category. Then there were the salient leaders, identified by outside observers as most powerfully influencing the group as a whole. The sociometric leaders were picked by other members of the group as being seen by them as the leaders. Lastly there were the elected leaders, who were picked by the group by election after experience together.

It would not be difficult to find other classifications of leadership, but it is probably sufficient when thinking of a class to distinguish between what Gardner (1956) has called functional leadership and popularity. Functional leadership denotes 'the actual exercise of leadership within a group, as distinct from eminence, popularity, headship (or authority), domination and representation'. There is, nevertheless, no reason for assuming that leadership and popularity, or, for that matter, any of the other qualities mentioned in this list, are incompatible. Indeed, it is doubtful whether children would accept a really unpopular member of the class as their leader whatever adults might do in particular cases. Partridge (1943) came to the conclusion that, among adolescents, 'the person who has the admiration of his peers usually has the stuff of which leadership is made'. Gardner himself found that there was a significant correlation between popularity and functional leadership among twelve-year-old boys, and Howell (1942) found a correlation of $+0\cdot96$ between leadership and social status among students.

It is probably true, however, that while a leader enjoys at least a fairly high degree of popularity, the popular child is not necessarily a leader. Indeed both Shoobs (1946) and Shears (1952) have found that the leaders chosen by children in a work situation are not the people whom the same children choose as their friends. This leads to the conclusion that leadership may be specific to the situation in which it arises. Stogdill (1948) pointed out that an adequate study of leadership must also involve a study of situations, since leadership is a relation between people in a social situation. Gibb (1947) went so far as to say that 'leadership is not a quality which a man possesses; it is an interactional function of the personality and of the social situations'. In a later article (1951) he expressed the opinion that whether a given individual assumes leadership or not seems to depend both on the nature of the situation and the attributes of the person, and that, according to the nature of the situation, qualities such as intelligence, acquired abilities, previous experience and personality traits can become attributes of leadership.

There is some evidence from other investigators in support of this view. Haythorn, Couch, Haefner, Langham and Carter (1956) used personality questionnaires to divide men students into groups according as they tended to be authoritarian or equalitarian in their characteristics. They were then set to work in groups of four on scripts for films on human relations skills, and differences between the leaders who emerged in the groups were noted. The leaders in the equalitarian groups were rated as significantly more secure in the experimental situation, more equalitarian in their attitudes and more sensitive to others, as showing a higher degree of leadership, greater effective intelligence and less striving for approval than those in authoritarian groups. Different kinds of leadership were associated with the different personalities of the members of the groups.

Leaders in different types of student activity were tested by Williamson and Hoyt (1952) with the Minnesota Multiphasic Personality Inventory. The activities considered included fraternity or sorority, religious, governing boards, political activity and publications. Men and women student leaders in political activities differed markedly from others on some scales, tending to be more unstable and neurotic, but other leaders differed less markedly. In some cases differences were found between the leaders of various organizations within the main categories, for example, different religious societies. There was some evidence that student leaders did differ from students in general, but other factors, such as age, might have affected this result.

The question arises as to whether leadership is specific in children's groups as well as in adult ones. Evidence produced by Shears (1952) suggests that this is not necessarily the case. He found that as children got older they became better able to distinguish both the requirements for leaders in a particular situation and the individuals who possessed those requirements. Among thirteen-year-olds the same leaders were chosen for both work and social situations, but among sixteen-year-olds there was differentiation. It is not safe to generalize about leadership among younger children from the results of studies carried out with adults or older adolescents as subjects. Both the ability to lead and the ability to choose leaders may develop with increasing age.

Fortunately there have been a large number of studies of the characteristics of leaders among children of different ages. It is doubtful whether one should talk about leadership with children of kindergarten age at all. They do not as a rule form very cohesive groups and such leadership as has been observed appears to be more in the form of domination. Northway (1943), reporting a study by Smith of the ways in which nursery school children tried to control one another, said that among the younger children the most marked tendency was to order one another about. Disapproval was used more frequently among the older children. Request and co-operation were noted in all age groups but more in the older than the younger. Suggestion, advice, permission and accusation were rarely used by any of the children. These results are taken as evidence of a decline in egocentricity as the children got older and developed an understanding of more social methods of control.

Among older children more definite leadership can be observed. Analysing a large number of studies of leadership, Stogdill (1948) concluded that a leader tends to exceed the average member of his group in such qualities as intelligence, scholarship, dependability, activity and social participation, knowing how to get things done, alertness to and insight into situations. Jennings (1943 and 1950) found that among adolescent girls leaders had greater insight than others into the needs of their fellows, and had greater emotional maturity. One result of this was that they could control their own moods and establish rapport with others. This is an important point and supports the suggestion that while leaders do usually excel in some ways, they do not as a rule differ very markedly from their followers. The person who does differ very markedly from the rest may find it difficult to communicate with them and they may find it difficult to communicate with him. Thus a child who is much older or younger than the others, or who is markedly more or less intelligent than they is quite likely not to be accepted as a leader in a group. This agrees with Hallworth's (1952) view that groups form around persons who embody the values of the members. No one who differed markedly from the rest would be able to occupy this position in relation to them. Support for this theory was also given by Martin, Gross and Darley (1952). In their study of college women, most of whom came from the middle classes, they found that the leaders tended to identify themselves with middle-class standards to a greater extent than did the rest of the group.

At the same time the leader must be able to contribute something that the group needs. Thus in a work group the leader is likely to be a child who is rather better at school work than the rest. In athletics he is likely to be more physically mature, and this was what Latham (1951) found among boys of thirteen and fourteen. On social occasions, as Shears (1952) found, the leaders are likely to be children with more social experience than others. The leader must be the person who knows how to get things done, and he must also set a standard of work or behaviour and both keep to it himself and make others do so.

Another characteristic of leaders appears to be sensitiveness to other members of the group and to their opinions. Chowdhry and Newcomb (1952) found that students perceived by others as leaders were significantly better at judging the opinions of their groups on issues relevant to the groups' interests than were non-leaders. This may be the reason why they became leaders or it may be the result of coming into contact, as leaders, with more people than others, and thus acquiring a superior knowledge of the views of the group. Leaders did not appear to be superior to others in judging opinion on issues which were not related to the interests of their group. The conclusion is that while ability to judge others' attitudes is a necessary condition for leadership, it is not a sufficient reason. This ability must be demonstrated in a specific group and developed in relation to the interests of the group.

This links with the question of the stability of leadership. The evidence seems to suggest that in a group of fairly long standing, once the leaders have emerged they are likely to continue to hold their positions, unless there is some radical change in the group. Edwards (1952) found that this was the case in a group of school prefects, who, originally acceptable to the other boys, became more acceptable during their year of office. Wurster and Bass (1953) organized discussion groups among students who did not know each other and leadership status was estimated by trained observers. After five months' acquaintance, ratings of leadership were obtained from the students themselves, and were found to correlate to an extent of $+0.47$ with the observers' estimates. Leadership was evidently established and observable on first acquaintance and remained fairly stable as acquaintance developed. Juola (1957) also studied students in leaderless discussion groups and found that measures of time spent talking were related to assessments of leadership, and that the tendency to participate was quite stable and probably reflected personality characteristics.

Ratings made at different times agreed closely and were highly reliable.

Whether people who have been leaders in school groups are likely to be leaders in later life is a different question. Stogdill (1948) has said that 'the evidence available suggests that leadership exhibited in various school situations may persist into college and into later vocational and community life'. He does, however, add that 'knowledge of the facts relating to the transferability of leadership is very meager and obscure'. More and more the view seems to be gaining ground that leadership is a function not only of the individual but also of the group and the situation. While it is possible to identify the leader in a particular group situation, it is less easy to foretell who will be the leader, yet that is the task of those who, in various fields, must select leaders for training. A now common method of solving this problem is to study the possible leaders in situations as nearly as possible analogous to those in which they would be required to function. This approach has been adopted by the Armed Forces and Civil Service Selection Boards.

In school the problem is less the selection of leaders than the setting up of situations in which potential leaders may realize and develop their talents. Shears (1952) drew attention to the small amount of responsibility which most children experience during their school life. The number of children who hold any formal office at all is usually small, and the majority are relegated to other roles. From among these others informal leaders may arise, but they are not usually recognized by authority and get little encouragement or training to develop their powers. This is a state of affairs which, in the interests of the community, should be remedied. If this is not done, the result is likely to be sheep-like crowds who do nothing in emergencies and are swayed by any demagogue or propagandist who takes it upon himself to act as leader.

It may be of interest here to consider in some detail the roles of those children in the classroom who are not, at any moment, leaders. It must not be assumed that they are all necessarily followers. In addition to the leaders there are likely to be in the group some who are supporting the leaders and actively forwarding the task in hand. Yet others, while taking little active

Leadership

part, will be acquiescing in what is being done. These two groups may justly be regarded as followers. There will, however, be others. There will be the children who are taking no part in what is going on, but are day-dreaming, or looking out of the window, or quietly doing something else. They are causing no trouble, but are simply withdrawing. Then there are those who are actively opposed to the purposes of the group, who make a nuisance of themselves and hinder progress. These are obstructionists and are destroying the work of others. All these must be taken into account in conducting or studying a group activity, and the leader will have to deal with them all and try to bring them into his orbit. No study of leadership is complete without some study of the activities of the members of the group who are not leaders.

An important concomitant of the study of leadership should be a consideration of the effect of being a leader on the individual concerned. It has been said that all power corrupts. Is this borne out by observations of leaders? Lieberman (1956) studied a group of factory workers of whom some were promoted to foremen and others elected as union stewards and found changes in their attitudes to the management and the union. Compared with a control group whose status was unchanged, the men who became foremen became more favourable towards the management, and those who became stewards became more favourable towards the union. When, as a result of a trade recession, some of the foremen reverted to their original status, they also tended to revert to their original attitudes. The results were less clear-cut in the case of those stewards who were not re-elected to office.

It is interesting to speculate on the effect on children of changes in their status in their own group. Edwards (1952) noted that among a group of secondary school boys a rise in class position and in social status seemed to go together, and that boys of low social status tended to fall in class position. Hallworth (1952) noted that a change in status was nearly always accompanied by a change in personality, the child who gained in status becoming more lively and the one who lost becoming subdued. He went so far as to suggest that individuals do, in fact, take on the characteristics expected of them by the group. If social status is a function both of group values and individual personality, it may also be true that personality is a function of status and of the values experienced in the group. It is difficult, therefore, to decide whether a change in role is due to a change in personality, or whether the change in personality is due to a change in role. Edwards (1952) thought that the boys in his group who were promoted to leadership positions gained little, since they were already successful academically and socially and were perceived to be so by the group. At the same time he admits that the academic success of these boys was greater than would have been expected for their intelligence. There seems to be little evidence to suggest that success in a group, as shown by an improvement in status, has any ill effects. Indeed the reverse appears to be the case.

Is training for leadership possible? The evidence that leadership is specific to a situation rather than general makes this seem doubtful. On the other hand, it should be possible to give children experience of a great many situations in which some of them can exercise leadership, and by varying the type of situation allow as many children as possible to develop and use their talents in this direction. This is one of the strong arguments for an activity curriculum, using the term in the wide sense. To concentrate on training an élite, such as the prefects in a school, seems bad policy. In ordinary life, countless situations arise where someone on the spot has to take the lead, and this will be done more effectively by people who have been allowed to exercise their powers as they grew up. The passive crowd, which watches while a child drowns, and the mob which follows any agitator, are less likely to exist if children from their earliest years have used their own initiative and their own powers of leadership. It is obvious from studies such as those of Shears (1952) and Pearce (1958), quoted in Chapter I, that the ability to take the lead where necessary is not confined to the few.

There is also the danger that where those who are considered possible leaders are grouped together only a few of them will in fact exercise their powers of leadership, and the majority will remain as supporters or followers. There is, however, the cheering thought that in this kind of situation those whom

66

earlier on we classed as obstructionists may exercise their powers by leading in another direction. Though this might not be a socially desirable situation, it would help to satisfy the needs of some of the group. If we do not provide children with means of satisfying their needs, they are apt to find their own ways of doing so, and this is as true in the sphere of leadership as in any other.

VI
PSYCHOLOGICAL CURRENTS AND EMOTIONAL STATES

PARENTS and teachers are well aware of the importance of fashion at some stages of children's development, when the wish to conform with accepted modes of behaviour, dress, speech and so forth is extremely strong, and the child who is different and knows it may suffer agonies of self-consciousness. The way fashions are established among children is one aspect of a more general phenomenon.

In any group it is a matter of common observation that ideas, opinions, information and habits spread among the members. An item of news will be passed from one to another and will be heard by a succession of people, each of whom is a link in a chain. Not all the members of the group will be affected in this way, but only those who are in contact with one another. These chain organizations within the group were noted by Moreno (1953) and called by him networks.

Moreno describes how an epidemic of running away occurred in a school for maladjusted girls and how he traced the network through which the idea of running away spread. It began with one girl and from her was taken up by others with whom she had contact, being passed on in turn by them and so affecting girls who seemed to be very far apart in the community. A study of the sociograms of the school brought to light a number of such networks, and their existence was verified by following the ways in which an artificially planted rumour ran through them.

The way in which a rumour spread through another community is described by Festinger and his associates (1947). The community this time was not a school but a low-rent housing project, in which community activities, including a nursery school, were being developed. The rumour suggested that the new activities were being developed by communists.

A study of the people who heard the rumour showed that some types were more likely to have heard it than others. They included people who participated actively in community life, and who had close friends, rather than people who had only aquaintances or no friends. It was found, too, that the people who heard the rumour were people to whom the information was likely to be relevant, in this case parents of children of nursery school age.

The authors lay down as a general principle that rumours will tend to arise where people have little control over developments which affect them. The spread of a rumour will depend upon the ease with which people can get in contact with one another, and so will be spread most widely by active members who have many contacts. The extent of the spread will be governed by the structure of the group and the patterns of communication within it. Bottlenecks may exist which will impede communication, or duplicated channels may assist it.

Longmore (1948) studied communication lines in a village community in Peru, which could be divided into three status groups. He found that the two lower ones tended to respond to the prestige of the highest group and that the lowest group responded to the other two. The intermediate group tended to receive a response from both the highest and the lowest, but the tendency was for a lower status group to try to associate itself with one of higher status. This corresponds with the kind of social climbing which can be seen in most communities.

The extent of this upward communication will vary from one person to another. Cohen (1958) brought together a group of students and created among them an artificial hierarchy, consisting of one high rank group and two low rank ones. For one of the latter upward mobility was possible, but not for the other, and it was found that those for whom promotion was possible tended to communicate with the upper group in ways

69

likely to protect and enhance their relations with them. The group for whom promotion was impossible had less need to behave in this way and consequently the high power group had less influence over them.

The direction in which communication flows was studied also by Bassett (1944), this time among a body of students. A sociometric test on three criteria showed a tendency for each student to make and/or receive a number of choices in one of thirteen cliques, which varied in size from seven to eighteen. Channels of influence were found between sixty-five of the possible seventy-eight pairs of cliques, and in twenty-six of these channels attraction flowed only in one direction, always towards the more popular clique. In thirty-nine of the channels attraction flowed both ways, but always the stronger current was towards the more popular clique. It was noted also that the popularity of a clique depended on the popularity of its most popular member.

Where there is no line of communication between groups there can be no flow of information between them. That groups do fall into separate sections is well known, and the phenomenon is called cleavage. The most obvious example of this is the way in which boys and girls separate out at certain ages. Among kindergarten children there is little consciousness of sex differences, but in the junior school years this increases and in early adolescence boys and girls rarely mix voluntarily. During later adolescence they come together again. Sociograms showing this sex-cleavage are given by Moreno (1953), but any teacher is well acquainted with its existence. Sometimes the sex-cleavage will occur only in one type of situation. Mensh and Glidewell (1958) found that among third-grade children it was evident in play choices but not others.

Cleavage may occur for a variety of reasons and not always for the expected ones. Faunce and Beegle (1948) observed young people of both sexes aged between fourteen and twenty-six in three farm youth camps, where work groups were chosen on a sociometric basis. The choices at the beginning of the camp showed a marked sex-cleavage, girls choosing girls and boys choosing boys significantly more often than would be expected by chance. The difference was significant at the 1%

level. A week later the choices had shifted so that they corresponded much more nearly with the chance pattern, and the suggestion is made that the original choices were made in conformity with a culturally expected pattern rather than with real preferences. The girls' preferences shifted more than did those of the boys.

Early in the camp there was a strong tendency for members to select as workmates others who came from their own part of the country rather than those who came from a different area. At the end of the week, when they all knew one another better, choices were more widely distributed and a large number went to new acquaintances. We have here the tendency to play safe and choose the familiar rather than be adventurous and choose the unknown.

Age, too, was important in the choices. Three groups were considered, those under eighteen, between eighteen and twenty-one, and twenty-one and over, the numbers in them being 34, 49 and 44 respectively. The oldest group strongly rejected both younger groups. The middle group tended to reject the youngest group but selected the oldest group more or less in accordance with expectations. The youngest group rejected the oldest group and made most of its choices within itself.

Cleavage can sometimes occur where a subgroup is maladjusted to the majority of the group. Kerstetter (1940) instanced such a case, where a subgroup of five boys was strongly rejected by the remainder of a fifth-grade class. As a result the subgroup withdrew into itself, giving all its choices to its own members. Tendencies to delinquency developed which were only checked when the teacher of the class broke up the group and the members were reabsorbed into the class. Here the teacher was aware of the situation and able to take appropriate therapeutic action. Blyth (1958) mentions a case where teachers were unaware of cleavage existing among junior school boys. Here there was no question of maladjustment, and the reason was simply that the boys differed in intelligence and interests and lived in different districts.

Personality differences sometimes cause cleavage. French and Mensh (1948) found that in a group of thirty-four women students, twenty-five formed a relatively well-integrated group

71

of whose members only one made a choice outside the group, and of whom all had at least one reciprocated choice within the group. Of their seventy-five rejections only twelve were within the group. The remaining nine students were relatively isolated. The majority group was subdivided for experimental consideration into those who did and those who did not receive rejections. When they rated themselves and the rest of the group on six personality traits, it was found that the members of the majority group who received no rejections were rated as superior in sociability, fairmindedness and sense of humour to those who received rejections, and were highest also on intelligence, punctuality and self-confidence. The minority group and the remainder of the majority group did not show any great differences in ratings, but the minority group rated itself higher than the other two on sense of humour.

Sometimes cleavages which might be expected are not found, especially among children. Sower (1948) found that in a suburban community, among seventh- to ninth-grade pupils, parental occupation had no significant influence on the children's friendship choices. Becker and Loomis (1948) found that in a school drawing on both rural and urban populations, cleavages between students coming from farms and those from the town did not exist. Personal qualities, values and moral standards displayed by pupils in their relations with one another, rather than whether they came from the town or the country, decided their friendship choices and accounted for rejections. This state of affairs, the writers think, was probably the result of determined efforts made at an earlier date to bring the farmers into the life of the town. The success of these efforts was reflected in the close integration of the children of rural and urban parents.

It seems likely that children make the friendship choices they do because of personal qualities rather than on a basis of socio-economic or other extraneous factors. Where children are rejected or cleavage occurs between groups in the classroom the reasons are likely to be found in the personalities of the children and their opportunities for meeting one another and sharing their interests and activities. It may sometimes happen that children of different social standings appear to shun one another and stick to friends of their own level, but this is frequently because families tend to be friendly with others of their own level, and so the children know one another better than they know children of other levels. As Becker and Loomis (1948) found, where children are given the opportunity to mix and choose their friends without differentiation between social classes, then children tend to ignore class levels in forming their friendships.

Criswell (1942) considered the way in which cleavage can occur between a majority and a minority group and she suggested that a small minority group will usually be assimilated into the majority group, but that if the number of minority members increases beyond a certain point then cleavage between the two groups will occur. The extent to which minority members are assimilated may vary from complete acceptance to complete rejection, and the point at which cleavage occurs may depend on the size of the group. In a group of ten, the introduction of two outsiders might be sufficient to produce it, but in a group of a hundred more than twenty might be assimilated without any break-up. It is suggested, too, that the rate at which the minority members are added to the group may have some effect. If they join in ones or twos, each addition may be assimilated before the next is made, and so far more may eventually be assimilated than would have been the case if larger numbers were introduced at one time. Teachers who have seen new children or strangers, such as refugees, enter a class during the term will bear out that small numbers are usually accepted by the other children without difficulty. This result may also be obtained because the strangers, being few in number, have little opportunity of forming a satisfactory separate group. Where there are more of them, cleavage may be as much due to their drawing together among themselves as to their being rejected by the majority.

The cohesiveness of a group depends upon the attitude of the members to one another. Berkowitz (1954) manipulated the cohesiveness of four groups of men students by telling them that they would probably like or dislike the groups with whom they would have to work. Actually the students worked at different tasks in different rooms and received notes telling them the

F

rate at which their supposed co-workers wanted them to work. Those who had had it suggested to them that they would like their co-workers were found to be more likely than the others to conform to the supposed group standard, and the conclusion is drawn that members of more cohesive groups are more likely to accept group standards than are members of less cohesive groups. In a highly cohesive group the probability is that there will be many channels of communication between members, so that ideas and standards are easily passed on, and the group standard may be much more definite and much better known to the members than would be the case in a more loosely-knit group. The attitude of the members which makes for greater cohesiveness is likely also to make the members more inclined to accept the group's standards, and the result is more homogeneous behaviour than would otherwise obtain.

Other influences which may affect groups and their members are emotional in origin. It would be idle to pretend that the work in most classrooms is carried out in an atmosphere free from emotional stress. Indeed it may be questioned whether any learning ever takes place unless the learner is in a state of tension which can be reduced by successful application to some task. The need to learn is itself an emotional state, and it is proposed to review some of the work which is concerned with the influence of various emotional states both on the structure of the classroom group and on the individuals composing it.

Probably the most common cause of emotion in any classroom is competition. Children compete against one another, with or without the encouragement of their teachers, and a number of studies have been carried out with a view to assessing the relative merits of methods of instruction based upon competition and co-operation. Most of these studies are concerned with the results of group methods of organization as opposed to more formal lecture methods. These are often described as student-centred and instructor-centred methods. Their results have been assessed both in terms of the knowledge gained by students and the effects on their personality and adjustment to the group.

Most workers seem to agree that there is little difference in the amount learned by students under the two methods.

74

Rasmussen (1956) organized university extension classes on both methods and found no significant differences between the two groups on a test of subject matter given six months after the course. Haigh and Schmidt (1956) obtained a similar result with college students. Blue (1958), on the other hand, suggests that all but exceptional students will probably improve their grades when studying in groups rather than individually.

Careful investigations of the value of group methods of instruction in schools were carried out by Richardson (1948) and Hallworth (1952). Both used control groups not taught by group methods for purposes of comparison, and observations were made over long periods, in the case of Richardson from January 1947 to October 1948 and by Hallworth from July 1947 to July 1950.

Richardson taught English composition by group methods to a class of girls during their first and second years in a grammar school. At the beginning of the experiment the class contained a large number of unresponsive children who rarely contributed voluntarily to the work in hand. The general attitude to the subject was poor, the group was badly integrated and there were many isolates. The class was divided up into work groups on the results of a sociometric test, using the criterion writing compositions together. During the course of the experiment the sociometric test was repeated at intervals, and it was found that in the experimental group the number of isolates fell more rapidly than in the control group, a parallel class which was given the sociometric tests but not taught by group methods.

Tests of attainment in English and in composition and a test of attitude to English composition were given to both groups. Both gained significantly in attainment during the experiment, and the experimental group gained significantly more than the control group in composition, the subject taught by group methods. The attitude of the experimental group to English composition also improved significantly, but this was not true of the control group.

As a result of her observations Richardson concluded that the ability to co-operate in group work depended less on the talents of individuals than on three factors.

1. The groups should be well-integrated socially and should want to work together.
2. The size of the groups should be appropriate to the task. For example, smaller groups are required for written work than for dramatic work.
3. It is important that the groups should contain individuals who can lead them. The best leaders were those who brought out the best in others and not girls who tended to dominate their groups.

In Hallworth's study the subjects were pupils in the first four years of a grammar school course. The school was a mixed one. Two parallel forms in the fourth year were taught geography by group methods, while a third form at the same level was used as a control group. No objective evidence was found of the influence of group work on attainment, but the majority of the children thought that they worked better and learned more quickly and more easily when in groups. The work took on the character of research rather than being an imposed task. There was, however, evidence of a more positive attitude towards geography as a result of the group method, and there was an improvement in the morale of the classes taught in that way. Co-operation between the children themselves, and between the children and the teacher, also improved.

There is evidence of differences in the adjustment of pupils resulting from competitive and co-operative methods of organization. Rasmussen's (1956) students estimated that they had learned more and had been more interested in what they learned in the student-centred groups, though in fact they did not display superior knowledge when tested. They also estimated that what they had learned would be of more practical use to them, that their attitudes had been changed and that, as a result, their behaviour would change. Deutsch (1949) found that there was greater personal insecurity and an interruption in the communication of ideas, as well as less friendliness, pride in the group, harmony and effectiveness, in competitive groups. Muller and Biggs (1958) also found evidence of freer and more spontaneous discussion in groups where the members had chosen one another as friends. In groups not formed in this way discussion was more formal and reserved. This may be linked with the increase in self-confidence and reduction in tension noted by Shoobs (1947) when a socio-metric method of grouping was used.

Phillips and D'Amico (1956), working with fourth-grade children, found that there was an increase in the cohesiveness of co-operative groups, but that competitive groups did not necessarily become less cohesive.

Wilkie (1955) experimented with fourth-year pupils in a junior school. They were divided into two groups, an experimental group which spent an afternoon a week on dramatic work and a control group which spent the same time doing normal class lessons in English. Both groups showed an improvement in mental ability and attainment, but the gains of the C-stream children in the experimental group were markedly greater than those of the ones in the control group. The experimental group seemed to get more satisfaction out of their contacts with other children, and the results of a *Guess-Who* test suggested that they were more aware of one another as persons than were those in the control group.

Results obtained by Bradburn (1954) and Gardner (1942) also point to the likelihood that infant school children taught by more informal and freer methods, allowing for considerable mixing and co-operation, are more emotionally secure and better-adjusted socially than children of the same age taught by traditional and more formal methods. Whether the long-term results of the two types of teaching differ significantly is in doubt, for the findings of a later inquiry by Gardner (1950) in which the subjects of her earlier study were re-assessed after some years were inconclusive. Unfortunately too many of the authors of studies of this type are committed to a theory and this affects to some extent their interpretations of their findings.

The weight of the evidence would appear to suggest that whereas co-operative groups do improve their adjustment, competition does not necessarily have bad effects. Phillips and D'Amico (1956) seemed to think that the effects of competition are not likely to be bad in cases where the groups are well-matched and as a result rewards are more or less evenly distributed. Haigh and Schmidt (1956) made the interesting suggestion that the capacity of students to respond to these two teaching methods depends on their personality qualities. If this is true, and it well may be, a judicious mixture of co-operation and competition might be the most effective method of dealing with most classes. At the same time it must be remembered that personality is to a great extent the result of the social climate in which the individual lives, and we might do well to heed Deutsch's (1949) suggestion that we should consider what types of personality we wish to produce and arrange the social climate of our classrooms accordingly.

Bound up with co-operation and competition are success and failure, and the influence of these conditions on individuals and groups merits serious consideration. In a competitive situation there must always be some who win and some who lose. Under co-operative conditions success and failure may be less marked for individuals. Nevertheless there will be, for nearly all pupils, occasions when they are unsuccessful at the task in hand, either in terms of an objectively demonstrable failure or by comparison with others who are more successful. It is probably these results of a competitive system which lead many educationists to deplore it, since they argue that the experience of failure, whether actual or comparative, is deleterious to children. In view of this it is surprising that there has not been more observation of the actual effects of success and failure.

The effects of success and failure may be observed in two fields. First, there is their effect on the subsequent performance of individuals, and second, there is their influence on the ways in which individuals form themselves into groups. An experiment by Tyler (1958) dealt with the first of these. In a laboratory experiment subjects were given the task of predicting which of a series of lights would be flashed. The lights were flashed according to a definite pattern and success was theoretically possible after three trials. After each prediction, one group of subjects was encouraged, another was discouraged, a third was sometimes encouraged and sometimes discouraged, while a fourth group was treated as a control and no comments were made on their performance. It was found that the control group performed as well as the group that was encouraged, and both these groups did better than either of the other two. The mixture of encouragement and discouragement had about the same effect as consistent discouragement. This makes it appear that discouragement has a more marked effect in inhibiting success than encouragement has in promoting it. If this is so, then it is more important for a teacher to avoid disparaging remarks than to give deliberate encouragement to pupils, a point that may be worth noting.

An interesting study of two grammar school C-streams was made by Pearce (1958). These, as the least successful forms in their year-group might be considered to be experiencing failure, at least by comparison with the more successful A- and B-streams. One form was taught by co-operative group methods in a number of subjects. The other was not. Tests showed a decline in morale and attainment in both forms over the first three years they were in the school, but this deterioration was markedly less in the form taught by group methods. As a result of his observations Pearce concluded that where streaming or anything else gave a sense of failure or a reputation for inferiority, it was inevitable that there should be a decline in morale, effort and attainment.

Whether children are successful or not may have an effect on the ways in which they form spontaneous groups in class. It has already been noted that academic success has an effect on sociometric status. Gilchrist (1952) studied groups of students engaged on a laboratory task where some were made to succeed and others to fail. They worked as individuals at first and then were asked to choose partners for similar work. It was found that both successful and unsuccessful subjects chose successful ones as partners. Subsequently some groups were made to succeed while others failed. When a second choice of partners was allowed it was found that those who had been successful both as individuals and in their groups tended to choose other similarly successful partners, but that those who had failed both as individuals and in groups tended to distribute their choices between those who had been successes and failures. The successful students seemed to be bound together by their success, but those who had failed were searching for a more satisfying partnership.

The effects of anxiety were studied by Ostlund (1956). A class of students who had been taught by a case-discussion method and had developed a high degree of integration was violently attacked by their instructor, who accused them of lack of preparation and irresponsibility in discussion. Their anxiety was heightened by threatening their academic standing. The ensuing discussion was recorded and it was found that, although the group demonstrated a high degree of integration, the standard of discussion was low. It was suggested that, as integration did not suffer, the discussion might have returned to a satisfactory level if the time allowed for it had been longer.

Halmos (1950) and Trent (1959) were concerned with the effects of anxiety on individual members of groups. Halmos found that students in a technical college who showed anxiety traits on a test of neuroticism also had a restricted social life, and that there were indications that the same was true of students who showed symptoms of depression. Trent found that among delinquent boys the less anxious were of higher socio-metric status than the more anxious. Although anxiety may sometimes be a spur to effort, there can be little doubt that it often has a bad effect on the confidence with which the individual approaches others, and it may also affect the quality of the performance both of individuals and groups.

The influence of different kinds of stress situations on the behaviour of student groups has been observed by Lanzetta (1955) and Hamblin (1958). Lanzetta gave groups of volunteers a reasoning and a mechanical assembly task and varied the conditions, so that some groups experienced a non-stress situation where there was no time-limit and no emphasis on the quality of their performance. Other groups were subjected to mild stress, where there was a time-limit and the time was called out at intervals. Yet others were subjected to severe stress, where they were badgered about their poor performance on the reasoning task, and made to work in a confined space and had the time allowed cut during the mechanical assembly task.

It was found that negative social and self-orientated behaviour decreased under increased stress, and that there was an increase in positive, group-orientated behaviour. Under stress the group became more friendly and co-operative and drew together, as though the members perceived it as a source of security in the face of external threat. The actual group performance was found to be best under mild stress.

Hamblin (1958) obtained a different result. His method was to set groups of adult subjects to play a ball game of which they had to discover the rules. A crisis was produced during the game by altering the rules. Half the groups experienced the crisis situation, and it was found that group integration decreased rather than increased during the crisis. Considering his own results and previous research, Hamblin suggests that group integration decreases during a crisis if there is no likely solution available, but that if a co-operative solution seems possible then group integration increases. Sometimes, however, a competitive solution may be possible and then the group is likely to disintegrate. This seems to be another way of saying that while on occasion there is safety in numbers, there are other occasions when every man for himself is best.

Frustration is an experience which comes to most people at some time. Its effect on groups has been studied by French (1944) and Wright (1943). French set groups of Harvard students to attempt the solution of insoluble problems, some of the groups being composed of students who were strangers to one another, and others of students who knew one another in some other context. He called these unorganized and organized groups, respectively. A wide variety of types of behaviour was observed in the groups. These included withdrawal from the group, playing with substitute problems, boredom, fatigue, aggressive behaviour, cheating, increased organization and co-operation, division of groups into factions, the development of scapegoats, and many more. There was more social restraint among the members of the unorganized groups, while the organized groups showed a stronger identification of members with the group and also more social freedom among themselves.

Wright (1943) observed the behaviour of children between the ages of three and six years who were first allowed to play with some toys which were then put out of reach. The children played in pairs, some of whom were described as strong friends, others as weak friends. The experiment is thus similar to that carried out by French, the difference being mainly in the ages of the subjects. It was found that the strength of the friendship affected the children's reactions to frustration. Strong friends showed more co-operation and less conflict, and also more violent aggression against the experimenter than did weak friends. There was also a regression in the maturity of the children's social behaviour. They became unhappy rather than happy, hostile rather than friendly to the experimenter, and there was a significant increase in destructive behaviour. Apparently reactions to frustration are much the same among children and adults.

A lack of efficient leadership can also lead to frustration in a group. This was demonstrated in the case of a group of children by Lippitt and White (1943), in a group of students by Hallworth (1957), and in a group of adults by Trist and Sofer (1959). In all cases frustration tended to find expression in aggression, either against the leader who refused to lead as the group thought he should, or against other group members. This type of frustration is apparently the result of finding oneself in a group whose structure is not clear, and in which the members feel insecure and uncertain of their own roles so that the cohesion of the group is reduced. It should be noted that Lippitt and White (1943) also found that a too autocratic form of leadership could also produce a reduction in cohesion by reducing the responsibility of the members for the group and making them apathetic. An alternative response noted in some groups was aggression in the form of rebellion, where the group showed increased cohesion in opposition to the autocratic leader. A fuller discussion of the effects on groups of different types of leadership will be given in a later chapter.

French (1944) also considered the reactions of his subjects to fear, which was induced by suffusing the room in which they were locked with smoke to simulate a fire. Behaviour varied from scepticism to panic. The organized groups showed more fear than the unorganized groups, possibly because the members of the organized groups were more closely bound together and so were more aware of one another's reactions.

It will be noted that many of these studies are concerned with laboratory situations. They deal with emotional states which can occur in classrooms and which do occur in some. The difficulty of making comparable observations in the classroom is the difficulty of providing comparable control situations, but any observations of this kind would be of immense value. We may not be justified in assuming that the effects of stress and crisis, failure and success, frustration and fear, would be exactly the same in classroom groups as they are in laboratory groups, but in the absence of other evidence we should accept the findings of these observers as indications of the kinds of effects we may reasonably expect. We are fully justified in asking whether these are the kinds of experiences to which we wish to subject our children.

VII

JUDGING OURSELVES AND OTHERS

THERE are a great many situations in daily life when we form, and sometimes express, opinions about other people. We form these opinions as a result of our observations of their behaviour, what we have been told about them by other people, and what they tell us about themselves. The opinions we form are important because they condition our behaviour towards other people, and this in turn conditions their behaviour.

The way other people behave towards us affects, among other things, the opinions we hold about ourselves and which we believe they hold about us, and these, again, help to determine the ways in which we behave and our reactions to other people. We all know that there are some people with whom we always feel at our best, while others seem to bring out all that is bad in us. In some groups we are happy and at our ease, in others we are gauche and uncomfortable. At the same time a frequently-quoted couplet suggests that our power of assessing our true effect on other people is very limited, and that, in fact, our picture of ourselves is very far from accurate.

The data on which we base our assessments of other people are varied. Sometimes they are a composite of impressions gathered over a long period of time in many circumstances. Sometimes they are based on isolated incidents which have impressed us strongly and which appear to be indicative of certain characteristics. Usually we form, fairly early in our acquaintance, certain views about people on to which we graft the results of closer acquaintance.

84

That strangers meeting for the first time do form definite opinions about one another was illustrated by Barker (1942). Twelve university students, six men and six women, who were complete strangers to one another, were asked at their first meeting to choose seat mates for the session and to fill in a *Guess-Who* test about one another. Stars, isolates and reciprocal pairs were found among this group of strangers, and the distribution of choices differed considerably from chance. Good looks seemed to be the quality most highly related to desirability. Young and Cooper (1944) found that among school children attractiveness of appearance was significantly related to popularity, and suggested that this is often a basis for initial popularity, which may be less likely to be displaced by subsequent differences in behaviour among children than among adults. Support for this view is given by some results noted by Kuhlen and Lee (1943). They found that among children between the ages of eleven and seventeen good looks were related to acceptability, but that the connection was less close among the older than among the younger children.

The use of leaderless discussion group techniques among strangers is based on the assumption that strangers take up positions relative to one another which are some indication of their future status. Wurster and Bass (1953) tested this proposition by comparing ratings given by trained observers of such a group with ratings of leadership status made later by the peers of the students concerned. They found a correlation of +0·47 between the two sets of ratings, and concluded that the leaderless discussion among strangers was as effective for predicting future status as is a similar discussion among friends.

Assessments of strangers must obviously be made from observation of superficial characteristics such as appearance and overt behaviour. Assessments of people who are better known can be made from a wider range of data. These are frequently expressed as ratings on specified personality traits, such as diligence, self-confidence and sociability. Sometimes the ratings are numerical and 5, 4, 3, 2, 1, or +2, +1, 0, −1, −2 are scales in common use, sometimes they are literal, A, B, C, D, E. The number of grades used depends on the purpose of the

85

rating or the amount of knowledge the raters have of the subjects. Five is a common number to use, since a greater number puts a strain on most people's powers of discrimination and fewer gives a rather coarse distribution. An odd number is usual, as this provides a middle or average grade.

Rugg (1922) has shown that to obtain the most accurate results it is necessary to average the ratings of several competent judges. He states that reliability increases with the square of the number of judges. Furfey (1926) has suggested, as an alternative to increasing the number of judges, increasing the length of the scale by dividing the traits into subtraits. Using this method of rating seventy-five boys on eighteen traits, he found a correlation of +0·888 between the ratings of two judges who knew the boys well. Furfey also reduced the ratings on the separate traits to standard scores, a precaution not always taken by workers in this field.

The difficulty of using such a scale lies in the varying standards of different raters, the different meanings they often attach to the trait names used, and the different ways in which they tend to distribute their ratings. If ratings by different raters are to be combined or compared, then they must be distributed in the same way if the results are to be statistically sound. This is sometimes achieved by suggesting a suitable distribution which conforms approximately to the normal curve.

e.g. A   B   C   D   E
      10   20   40   20   10% of the group.

A graphic rating scale as described by Freyd (1923) is often used and gives good results. Here a line, sometimes divided into sections, sometimes with only the ends labelled with extreme expressions of the quality under consideration, is marked at a point which, in the opinion of the rater describes the subject most accurately. The distance of this mark from one end of the line can then be measured off and used as a rating of the subject.

e.g. ———————————————————X————————

Very self-confident   Very diffident

Another grave disadvantage of the use of rating scales where subjects are to be rated on a number of qualities is the existence of *halo*. This is the tendency of raters to form a general opinion of each subject and to make all trait ratings in the light of this. The result is that a subject of whom the rater has a good opinion is likely to be rated high on all desirable traits and low on all undesirable ones. The reverse is true in the case of a subject of whom the rater disapproves. This tendency can be overcome to some extent by warning raters of the danger and asking them to rate all the subjects on one trait, then proceed to rate them on another trait, and so on, instead of rating each subject in turn on all the traits.

In spite of their disadvantages ratings are useful in that they make it possible to obtain fairly quickly and easily the opinions about the subjects of a number of observers. Vernon (1953) reports a validity of $+0.60$ for ratings as compared with co-efficients for objective tests of between $+0.30$ and $+0.45$. This is some justification for the continued use of ratings, at least in conjunction with, if not instead of, more objective tests. Their use is likely to continue anyway, if only because so many people have more faith in personal judgments than in objective tests.

When attempting to get peer-ratings from children, rating scales are less suitable than with adults. Children are less able to distinguish the qualities under consideration, though, as Shears (1952) found in the case of leadership, this increases as they get older. A more suitable method with children is the *Guess-Who* technique. Here short character sketches of children showing varying degrees of the qualities to be rated are drawn up and the children are asked to guess which members of the class they describe. In this way ratings on a variety of qualities can be obtained, which are samples of the reputation of different pupils in the eyes of the class. These can be compared or combined with ratings made by teachers or the results of objective tests.

People vary very considerably in their ability to judge others. Vernon (1953) cited evidence that good raters tend to be above average in intelligence and maturity. Most people are more successful in judging others who are in some way like themselves, in sex, age, or cultural background. They are also better at judging traits which they themselves possess in a high degree, providing these are desirable traits. This is not true in the case of undesirable traits. The confidence with which a rater records a judgment is no guarantee of its accuracy.

Ratings made by an individual of his own qualities suffer from all the defects which affect ratings made by others. The honesty with which self-ratings are made depends on the circumstances and on whether anything important depends on the result. The picture an individual has of himself may differ considerably from the picture others have of him. Shen (1925) investigated the validity of self-estimates made by a small group of men, who ranked themselves and one another on eight traits. He found that they ranked themselves less accurately than they ranked one another, but that errors of self-estimate made by any individual were likely to be systematic. Some people tended to over-estimate, others to under-estimate themselves on most of the traits considered. Shen suggested that although individuals do not rank themselves very accurately in a group, they nevertheless know themselves well in the sense of knowing their relative strengths and weaknesses rather accurately. It should be noted that none of the traits Shen investigated were derogatory. In general, the usual opinion is that individuals tend to over-estimate themselves on desirable traits and to under-estimate themselves on undesirable ones.

The concept of the self has long been of considerable interest to psychologists, and the term is used in two quite distinct ways by them. It may mean the person's attitudes and feelings about himself, or it may be thought of as a group of psychological processes which govern the individual's behaviour and adjustment. This is not the place for a lengthy account of theories of the self. For a succinct review of a number of these theories the reader is referred to Hall and Lindzey (1957).

Whether there is such a thing as a 'real self' is open to question. If there is, it is difficult to see how any mortal can arrive at an estimate of the 'real self' either of himself or anyone else. It is convenient to distinguish a variety of pictures of the self. There is, for example, the self as seen by the individual himself. This may or may not correspond to the self as seen by others, and this, in turn, may depend on who those others are. Friends and enemies, superiors and subordinates, may have various estimates of an individual. Then there is the self as the individual believes others see him, which may or may not have the characteristics they really attribute to him. It would be easy to extend this list of selves very considerably.

Brownfain (1952) investigated the relations between some of these selves. He asked sixty-two men students at the University of Michigan to fill in a self-rating inventory in four different ways. First he asked them to rate what he described as the 'private' self. Secondly to rate the 'positive' self, which he described as the self as hoped for with all reasonable doubts slanted favourably. Thirdly, to rate the 'negative' self, in which all doubts were slanted unfavourably to give a picture of the self as it was feared to be. The fourth self was the 'social' self, the self as each thought the other members of the group saw him. From these ratings a stability index was obtained for each individual by summing without regard for sign the differences between the positive and negative self-ratings. The sum of the differences between the ratings of the private self and the social self was used as an index of social conflict.

The results showed that subjects with stable self-concepts were better adjusted than those with unstable self-concepts. They had a higher mean self-rating and a higher rating on self-acceptance. They were freer of inferiority feelings and nervousness, and were better liked by the group and were considered more popular. They saw themselves more as they believed others saw them, knew more people in the group, and were themselves better known by the group. They were more active socially and showed less evidence of compensatory defensive behaviour.

A rather similar inquiry was carried out by Fiedler, Warrington and Blaisdell (1952), but in this case an attempt was made to link the subjects' descriptions of themselves with the accuracy of their perceptions of the self-feelings of others. Here a small group of students was asked to use a rating scale (1) to describe themselves, (2) to describe how they would ideally like to be, (3) to predict how their best-liked fellow group members would describe themselves, (4) to predict how their least-liked fellow group members would describe themselves.

It was found that the subjects perceived the fellow group

members whom they liked most as being more similar to themselves than those they liked least, and also as being nearer to their ideal selves than were the disliked ones. There was no evidence that the self-descriptions were actually more similar to the self-descriptions of the liked than the disliked fellows. Neither was there any evidence that relatively liked members perceived other members of the group in a different way from that of the relatively disliked members.

This links with a finding by McIntyre (1952) that in a large group of men students the mean sociometric scores of highly and poorly accepted groups on both acceptance-of-self and acceptance-of-others scales did not differ significantly. No support was found for the view that better interpersonal relations were a function of better attitudes to oneself and to others.

Northway and Wigdor (1947), on the other hand, found that a group of eighth-grade pupils of high sociometric status showed greater sensitivity than others of lower status in sensing the feelings of others, and a conscious striving for the approval of others. As indicated by the Rorschach Test, the intermediate group seemed to be more shallow and less introspective than either the high or the low status group, but they were able to see situations as others did sufficiently to be accepted to a degree that satisfied their needs for social interaction. Both the high and the low status groups deviated from normal on the Rorschach Test more than did the intermediate group, but the disturbances seemed more serious in the unaccepted group. Patterns of disturbance differed too. Among the unaccepted recessives, symptoms tended to be schizophrenic, whereas in the accepted group they were more often psychoneurotic.

To most people, and especially to adolescents, what other people think about them is important, and there have been a number of attempts at assessing the accuracy with which we can gauge the feelings of others towards us. Sociempathy, an individual's awareness of his own and others' social status in a given group of which he and they are members, has been investigated in relation to a number of other qualities. Ausubel (1955) found that in a large group of boys and girls of mean age 16·2 years, the sociometric status of the perceiver was not significantly related to accuracy of perceiving his own or others' sociometric status, but that the ability to perceive sociometric ratings received from others varied directly with the sociometric status of the raters. In other words, members of the group knew more accurately the opinions held about them by others of high status than they did the opinions of those of low status. This may mean only that the opinions of high status members of the group on most topics are generally better known to others than are the opinions of low status members.

Other writers, notably French and Mensh (1948), have found little relation between sociometric status and the individual's ability to perceive his own status. Trent (1959) found that in a group of delinquent boys in a training school, anxiety as measured by the Children's Form of the Manifest Anxiety Scale was negatively related to the boys' accuracy of perception of their own status. The less anxious boys tended to be of higher social status than the more anxious and had a more accurate perception of their own status. Whether the anxiety was a result of the low status or vice versa is not indicated.

It has been suggested that where the members are strongly attracted to a group, its standards of beliefs and behaviour are accepted as personal levels of aspiration, and that non-conformity with the group's ideals will come to seem as failure. The stronger the attraction of the group, the greater will be the feelings of inadequacy of those who fail to comply with its standards, and the stronger will be the feelings of success of those who win the group's approval. Evidence in support of this is adduced by Festinger, Torrey and Willerman (1954) and Rasmussen and Zander (1954). This suggests that the anxiety noted by Trent (1959) on the part of the boys of low sociometric status was a result of their failure to win greater approval from their fellows.

That there is a connection between personality adjustment and sociometric status is shown also by Grossman and Wrighter (1948) and Baron (1951). These investigators used self-rating personality inventories to measure the adjustment of their subjects and related the opinions of the subjects about their own personalities to their sociometric status, a measure of the opinions held about them by others. Grossman and Wrighter found that children who were rejected by the group reported more nervous symptoms than others and lacked a feeling of belonging, whereas those who were highly accepted had a more normal personality adjustment. Baron found that while girls of high status seldom indicated the presence of adverse emotionality or a sense of inordinate environmental demands, girls of low status frequently indicated both. The latter also compared themselves unfavourably with others and reported a sense of failure of accomplishment.

Bedoian (1953) administered a mental health questionnaire and a sociometric test to sixth-grade pupils, and reported that pupils whose sociometric status was high had better mental health than those who were ignored, unwanted, or disliked. Stars also appeared to have better mental health than the remainder of the class. Kuhlen and Bretsch (1947), too, noted that unaccepted children reported more personal problems than others and were aware of their lack of status. They stressed the importance of social skills to adolescents, and the fact that unaccepted children have their social inadequacy brought home to them daily, both at home and at school.

There can be little doubt that the children and young people who were the subjects of the above-mentioned studies were consciously or unconsciously aware of their own sociometric standing in the groups to which they belonged. High standing was generally associated with confidence and good mental health, low standing with worry and anxiety. In some cases the worries were admitted in responses made to mental health questionnaires, in others they became apparent through less direct admissions, such as responses to the Rorschach Test. The question always arises as to whether the poor social adjustment or the poor mental health is primary, but there seems to be a good case for assuming that help in improving the social standing of young people is in many cases likely to be associated with an improvement in mental health. Where a child or young person does not seem to be making a good social adjustment to his group, there is good reason for inquiring whether this may be either the cause or the result of unsatisfactory mental health and taking appropriate action to ease the situation.

The studies considered so far have been concerned with the awareness individuals have of their own sociometric status and with the effects of their knowledge. It is pertinent to inquire how much individuals know about their other qualities, such as social skills, intelligence and level of achievement. Bretsch (1952) obtained from 696 boys and girls, aged about fourteen and a half, estimates on a four-point scale of their level of performance in eight social skills, viz., dancing, swimming, tennis, skating or skiing, playing cards, singing, playing an instrument and carrying on a conversation. They were then divided into three levels of social acceptance on the results of a sociometric test involving six criteria, and extreme levels were compared on their ratings of their own performance and the extent to which they participated in the activities concerned. It was found that, in general, there was a low, significant, positive relationship between social acceptance and number of activities participated in. A greater percentage of the well-accepted than the poorly-accepted rated their own performances as average or above, and there was some agreement between their judgments and those obtained from their peers by means of a *Guess-Who* test. At the same time, differences between the sexes were greater than differences between the high and low social acceptance groups. On five of the eight skills, a greater percentage of girls than boys rated their performances as average or above.

Knowledge of social skills, which affect social acceptance, may possibly be more accurately assessed because of this than such qualities as intellectual level and academic performance. Torrance (1954) asked 1215 freshmen entering Kansas State College to estimate how they would stand in relation to their classmates on tests of general scholastic ability and achievement, and found little relationship between their estimates and their achieved standing. Over 65% estimated themselves in the top fourth on scholastic ability and 95% in the upper half. Of those who achieved results in the bottom fourth, 62% estimated themselves in the top fourth and 92% in the upper half. Re-estimates made after the tests were taken were more realistic. Women were much more realistic in their estimates than men but were more likely to under-evaluate their performance.

There was little to choose between the accuracy of prediction of those who did well and those who did badly on the tests. The lowest 25% expected to do as well as the highest 25%. Those who made the most serious miscalculations were said to suffer socially, economically, emotionally and sexually from an exaggerated sense of vulnerability. From this it would seem that accuracy of self-estimate is related to mental health.

Similar results were obtained by Arsenian (1942), who found that freshmen's estimates of their abilities, knowledge and interests did not correspond with their actual possession of those attributes as measured by objective tests. Again estimates were toned down after taking the tests and came nearer to the correct placement. Students who made gross over- or under-estimates were as a group less intelligent and less well-adjusted than the others and provided a disproportionately high number of problems during their subsequent college careers.

That the accuracy of self-knowledge can be improved is shown by the results of a study by Johnson (1953). Here the subjects were not children or students, but men between the ages of sixteen and thirty-eight who attended a vocational counselling centre. Before, immediately after, and one month after receiving guidance they were asked to estimate which fifth of the population they were in on a series of intelligence, personality and interest tests which were administered to them. It was found that vocational counselling significantly increased the accuracy and certainty of their self-knowledge, and that the gains were maintained to a high degree in the subsequent month. The greatest gains were in self-knowledge of the more objective qualities, intelligence and interests, and least in the realm of personality.

A different type of inquiry was carried out by Forrester (1951). This was concerned, not with awareness of their present status, but with the awareness of their own development shown by adolescents. Of the 293 boys and girls tested, all were conscious of some kind of development, intellectual, social, or spiritual, and all were conscious of a desire to develop. Not all wanted to develop in the same direction, but Forrester suggested that this universal desire for development means that 'there is no child about whom a teacher need despair, no child without something in him that will respond if he is given the opportunity to fulfil his ambition. Even if there is only one way in which a child really desires to develop, that can be a growing point for desire for development in other directions, and the child who is ambitious to develop in many ways is one who will be eager to make the most of all the opportunities offered to him'. The results of this study suggest that adolescents pay more attention to the opinions of adults than is sometimes thought, and this implies that they are aware of those opinions.

In many of the studies quoted members of groups were asked to compare their own status with that of others, a process which involves making assessments of the status of others. How accurate are these assessments? Ausubel (1953) obtained ratings of the popularity of their classmates from one hundred junior and senior high school boys and girls and compared the results with those of a sociometric questionnaire. He found no relationship between the sociometric status of the children and their predictions of the status of others. This result was supported by a later one, also reported by Ausubel (1955), though in this there was also evidence that the accuracy with which boys and girls perceive the sociometric status of others varies directly with the status of the others. They are more aware of the status of very popular members of the group than of that of those who are average or below average in status. No evidence was found that adolescents can most accurately perceive the sociometric ratings of others whose degree of popularity equals their own.

Trent (1959) attempted to relate the accuracy with which delinquent boys perceived their own status with their perception of the status of others, and found no significant correlation between the two. He suggested that the ability to perceive one's own status and the ability to perceive the status of others are separate, and involve different perceptual functions, and that whereas an individual's own feelings and emotions influence his perception of himself, he can view the status of others with greater objectivity. This was supported by his finding that, although anxiety was negatively related to the boys' accuracy of perception of their own status, it was unrelated to their accuracy of perception of the status of others.

That there may be a general ability to judge the status of

others is supported by Gronlund (1956). One hundred and seventy-six student teachers judged the sociometric status of their classmates and of these thirty also judged the status of their pupils. The correlation between the accuracy of their assessments for the peer and pupil groups was significant at the 1% level. There was no difference between the accuracy of their assessments of the status of boys and girls among their pupils, and accuracy was not affected by the size or age level of the class. In judging their peers, there was a tendency to assume a greater similarity between their own sociometric preferences and those of the group than in fact existed, but mean correlations between actual and assessed status ranged from +0·37 to +0·68.

That perceptions of personality and other qualities vary from one assessor to another is a matter of common observation. Robson (1918) asked twenty-one girls, all living in the same house, to rate themselves and their associates on a number of personality traits and found considerable differences between the ratings given by different people. In this case the ratings were all made by people of more or less the same standing. Differences may be expected to be even greater where the people concerned differ considerably from one another and also from those they are rating. An experiment of this kind was carried out by Evans (1952a).

Four personality qualities, self-confidence, fluency, sociability and resourcefulness were chosen for experiment. The subjects were twenty-two women students in a training college and each student was rated on these qualities, using a graphic rating scale, by members of the college staff who knew her well, by other students in the group, and by herself. The resulting ratings were intercorrelated and the results are given below.

Table 2. Correlations between personality ratings made by different groups

Groups	Self-confidence	Fluency	Sociability	Resourcefulness
Staff-student	+0·45	+0·61	+0·62	+0·64
Staff-self	+0·31	−0·07	+0·31	+0·52
Student-self	+0·17	−0·04	+0·39	+0·39

It will be noted that the correlations between ratings made

by the two groups of other people, the staff and the other students, are considerably higher than those between the self-ratings and the ratings made by either the staff or other students. This suggests that the impression made on the outside world has a certain amount of consistency, but that it may differ considerably from the impression the individual has of herself. This is more marked in the case of some qualities than others. Here the individuals' views of their own fluency differed more markedly from the views of others than was the case with resourcefulness. In the cases of self-confidence and resourcefulness the staff evidently agreed more closely with the students' assessments of themselves than did other students, while there was no such disagreement where sociability was concerned. This is likely to be due to the fact that staff and students see individual students in different situations and their opportunities of judging some qualities may be different. Opportunities for judging other qualities may be similar for both staff and other students. Whatever the causes, there is evidence here that there are definite variations in the judgments of personality made by different groups of people and by the people who are themselves being assessed.

Buchheimer and Pendleton (1954) carried out a very similar experiment in relation to group participation. The subjects again were students and this time a *Guess-Who* test was used. A moderate but definite agreement was found between teachers' and students' perceptions of effective participation in a classroom group, and self-perceptions of social adequacy tended to agree with those of other students.

The suggestion is made by Amatora (1955) that children's ratings of themselves should be validated by correlation with ratings made by other children rather than with ratings made by teachers or other adults. Adults and children may have different points of view and what should be considered is the impression made on peers rather than the impression made on an older generation. She compared ratings of self and peers made by two hundred boys and two hundred girls in grades four to eight on twenty-two personality qualities. There was considerable agreement between the two sets of ratings both for boys and girls, and the conclusion drawn was that the

97

child's own view of himself corresponded with the judgments of his overt behaviour made by his peers.

Both the impressions made on others and the view an individual holds of himself are important. The impression made on others will determine their reactions towards the individual, and the view he holds of himself will condition his approach to the outside world. Happiness or unhappiness, a good or poor adjustment, depend on the results of these.

As well as forming opinions about their fellows children also form opinions about their teachers, and it is probable that they have more chances of studying their teachers than of studying some of their fellows. A child is of necessity brought into contact with his teachers, but he may never have any close contact with a child who sits on the far side of the room from him, who lives in a different neighbourhood and comes to school by a different route, and who plays in a different group in the playground. Children who are in the same class may, apart from the fact that they know one another's names and appearances, be to all intents and purposes strangers. It might, therefore, be expected that children would make better ratings of their teachers than of their fellows. It might also be expected that the pupils of any teacher would have more accurate opinions about him than would other teachers or administrators who could see at most only occasional samples of his work in the classroom. This point of view has been held by a number of investigators who have used ratings obtained from pupils as measures of the efficiency of their teachers.

Evidence as to the reliability of pupil ratings of teachers is given by Bryan (1937), by Heilman and Armentrout (1936) and by Cook and Leeds (1947). Bryan, working with 1500 junior and senior high school pupils, reports reliabilities ranging from +0·61 to +0·97. Heilman and Armentrout, who administered the Purdue Rating Scale for Instructors to 2115 college students in the classes of forty-six teachers, found a reliability of +0·75. Cook and Leeds examined ratings by at least twenty-five pupils of each of one hundred teachers, and found an odd-even reliability of +0·94.

Investigations have been made of the influence of various factors on pupil ratings of teachers. It might be expected that

98

pupils who got high marks would rate their teachers higher than would pupils who got low marks. Blum (1936) found that this was not the case with college students. Students' ratings of the instructors did not depend on their own grades. Bryan (1937) found that there was a slight tendency for children who received high marks to rate their teachers higher than did children who received low marks, but there were exceptions to this. In the main the evidence suggests that students' grades have very little influence on their ratings of their teachers.

Brookover (1945) found that teachers having closer relations with their pupils were considered both by their pupils and by their employers to be better teachers. This agrees with the finding that people tend to rate more highly those with whom they are better acquainted.

The age and sex of teachers does not seem to have much influence on pupil ratings. Evidence on this point was given by Brookover (1940), Bryan (1937), and Herda (1935). Bryan found that boys tended to rate men teachers higher than girls do, while girls tended to rate women teachers higher than boys do. Herda found that where there was a difference it was in favour of the men, but such differences were not general. Brookover found no such distinction.

It is unlikely that any responsible person would be willing to accept the opinions of pupils as the sole criterion of a teacher's efficiency. The pupils may see most of the game, but they have not the knowledge to judge of the ultimate value of any teacher's work. There is usually, however, some correlation between assessments of their teachers made by pupils and by other observers.

Boardman (1928) intercorrelated ratings of 157 teachers made by supervisors, fellow teachers and pupils, and obtained coefficients ranging from +0·563 to +0·684. It is suggested that the lack of agreement may be due to the fact that each group has knowledge not possessed by the other two. Bryan (1937) reported that agreement between ratings of teachers made by different groups of pupils was greater than that between ratings made by pupils and administrators. He says that ratings made by administrators show more similarity from item to item than ratings made by pupils. This suggests that

99

the halo effect is more marked in the ratings of administrators than in those of pupils.

The study by Brookover (1945) mentioned earlier used pupil gains in history as the criterion of teaching efficiency. It was found that although teachers having closer relations with their pupils were considered both by their pupils and their employers to be better teachers, they were, in fact, less effective teachers of history. Pupil ratings of teaching ability had a low and somewhat inconsistent relationship with teaching effectiveness as measured by pupil gains in information. Employers' ratings showed no such relationship.

These findings suggest that pupil opinion of teachers is worth consideration in making an assessment of teaching efficiency. Bryan (1937) claims that pupil ratings are a valid measure of teacher merit to the extent that this is determined by the teacher's ability to impress pupils favourably. Cook and Leeds (1947) go farther and state the opinion that pupils' attitudes to teachers are the result of teachers' attitudes to pupils, and assume that the teacher who is liked by pupils and who has harmonious working relations with them has a high level of desirable personality traits.

VIII

TEACHERS AND PUPILS

IN studying the classroom group it is easy to forget that the teacher is a member of the group just as much as any of the pupils. The observer sees the group from an adult vantage point and observes often in the role of teacher, omitting to include in his observations the bonds that unite teacher and pupils or the rejections that separate them. Yet the teacher does not merely manipulate the group; he or she is part of it and affects and is affected by the currents of feeling that flow between the members. Sociometric studies of teaching situations cannot take this into account, for choices of companions for classroom activities cannot be directed to the teacher, who must of necessity remain outside all work groups while maintaining contact with them as director or adviser. Other methods must therefore be used in the study of teacher-pupil relations.

It would be difficult to over-estimate the importance of the influence which a child's teacher can exert over his character and mind. As English and Pearson (1947) have pointed out, most people want to have heroes, and, after his parents, his teacher is the person best placed to fill this role for a child. A good teacher, quite apart from the knowledge he or she imparts, has a profound effect on the personality development of the pupils. So has a bad teacher, and these writers hold that where a child shows an educational difficulty among the things that should be investigated are the attitude of his teacher and the relationship between teacher and child. Figueroa (1955) stressed the fact that education springs from the attitude of the teacher to his pupils, and that the problem of the right attitude is central in teaching.

What should this attitude be? Not purely an intellectual relationship, but one in which the pupils are accepted as persons in their own right, with their own needs and with a contribution to make to their own education. The importance of the I-thou relationship must be realized by the teacher, so that the children are never regarded as a means to satisfying his own needs for recognition or affection, and so that the teacher may be able to extend his influence to include children of all types, the isolate as well as the star.

How the teacher's own needs can affect the quality of his teaching is discussed by Myers (1916). Teachers, like everyone else, want to be liked, and in extreme cases this may lead insecure teachers to accept poor work and low standards of classroom behaviour. They may also try to impress their pupils with their knowledge and fail to reach the level of the child. Unintentional favouritism may result from the teacher's tendency to form attitudes to the pupils early in the course, and to react favourably to those pupils found most pleasing. Symonds (1950) observed that the most successful teachers are usually secure and confident, they are interested in and like children, and are able to accept them. In this the sincerity of the teacher is important, for though he may learn to disguise his feelings these are usually apparent to the children. Often the personality of the teacher can best be studied by observing the reactions of the pupils.

This is supported by the results of a study made by a team of observers led by Anderson (1945 and 1946). Two types of teacher behaviour were studied in ordinary classroom situations and the effects of these on the behaviour of the children were noted. One type of behaviour described as domination was 'characterised by a rigidity or inflexibility of purpose, by an inability or unwillingness to admit the contribution of another's experience, desires, purpose or judgment in the determining of goals which concern others'. It involved the attempt to impose one's own standards and purposes on others with consequent frustration of their aims. The other type, called socially integrative behaviour, involved co-operation in the pursuit of a common purpose, and the resolving of conflict rather than its augmentation or incitement.

At some time all the teachers observed provided examples of both these types of behaviour, but their relative amounts varied from one teacher to another. With most domination exceeded integration, and this was especially true when the contacts were with groups rather than with individual children. The time of day and the stage of the term had some effect on the amount of domination used, and this increased during the afternoons and as the term went on, but in spite of this individual teachers showed definite patterns of behaviour which were evidently habitual.

It was found that there were marked differences in the behaviour of the children under different teachers. Where the teachers used less domination and more integration the children were more attentive and co-operative, they were less restless, contributed more to the lesson, and showed greater spontaneity and initiative. The observers had little doubt as to which type of behaviour on the part of the teacher was more beneficial to the children.

The psychological climate of the classroom was not, however, necessarily the same for all the children, since it was observed that there was a tendency for the teachers to dominate some children more than others. Some children were aggressive and dominative in their approach to other children and these were met by domination from their teachers, so that a vicious circle was set up. Boys, too, were often dominated more by their teachers than girls.

Inevitably the question arose as to who initiated behaviour, the teacher or the children, since it might be argued that the behaviour of the teacher was adapted to meet the situations arising from the behaviour of the children. To settle this point the same children were observed a year later, by which time they had moved up and had new teachers and their former teachers had new classes. It was found that the behaviour of the teachers was substantially the same as it was originally, but that after a short period of adaptation the behaviour patterns of the children had changed to correspond with those of their new teachers. There was little room for doubt that the behaviour of the children was a response to that of their teachers, and not vice versa.

The well-known study by Lippitt and White (1943) also showed the effect of teacher behaviour on that of the children. This time the activities were not those of the ordinary classroom but were carried out by groups of five ten-year-old boys. Four such groups were selected, whose members were matched on the results of a classroom sociometric study, teacher ratings on social behaviour, observations in school and playground and school records of intelligence, physical status and socio-economic background. The groups engaged in what were described as 'club activities' under three different types of adult leadership, authoritarian, democratic and laissez-faire. The authoritarian leader decided himself what the group should do, how it should be done, and how the work should be divided among the members. He remained aloof from the group, except when demonstrating, and when he praised or blamed this was done on the basis of his own subjective judgment. The democratic leader encouraged discussion of the task and of the methods to be used. A choice of methods was given and group members allocated the work among themselves and decided which members should work together. Criticism was expressed in terms of objective standards and the leader was in spirit a member of the group, though he refrained from doing too much of the work himself. The laissez-faire leader left the group entirely free to make its own decisions without guidance from him. He supplied materials and information when asked to do so, made no comments on the progress of the work, and did not participate at all. At the same time he was friendly rather than unfriendly.

To eliminate the effects of the personalities of the leaders, each leader in turn assumed each type of leadership, and the groups experienced each type in turn. It will be seen that this differed from the study made by Anderson, where the work was that of the normal classroom and the teachers behaved according to their normal practice. In the experiment carried out by Lippitt and White observations were made of a series of planned and at least partially controlled situations.

Records of the behaviour of the four groups showed that the boys reacted quite differently to the three types of control. Autocracy provoked one of two reactions, submission or aggression which might amount to open rebellion. Group morale, in the sense of spontaneous cohesion or we-thinking, was highest in the democratic group and lowest in the submissive autocracy. The democratic group was the most friendly and contented, but autocratic leadership seemed to inhibit the normal free-and-easy sociability of the boys. The best work was done in the democratic group, who took a pride in their work in marked contrast to the lack of care shown by the autocratic group. The laissez-faire group were dissatisfied with their own level of efficiency and their behaviour showed the vicious circle of frustration-aggression-frustration. That they needed a clearer structure was shown by the way in which one of the boys attempted to take over the leadership of the group when the leader temporarily went out of the room.

In these studies various aspects of the influence of teachers on their pupils are touched upon, and some of these require fuller consideration. The achievement in school work, attitudes and emotional adjustment of the children are all likely to depend to a greater or lesser extent upon the characteristics and behaviour of their teachers. This has been most clearly recognized in the case of achievement, and attempts have been made to assess the efficiency of teachers in terms of the amount of knowledge of subject matter their pupils have gained from them. Where these assessments have been matched against other measures of teacher-efficiency the correlations have usually been low (Evans, 1951), and this is not surprising when one considers all the other factors (intelligence, health, home conditions, previous teaching, will to learn, etc.) which help to determine the amount any child learns in school. Arvidson (1956) is probably right in claiming that the ability of the teacher plays a relatively small part in the academic success of his pupils but may have a more marked effect on other aspects of child development.

There is some evidence that teachers can make a significant contribution to the emotional adjustment of their pupils. Flory, Alden and Simmons (1944) have described how twenty-three

H   105

maladjusted children, instead of being given specialist treatment, were left in the care of their own teachers. The children were all of normal intelligence and achievement and so presented a psychological rather than an educational problem. Over a period of two years all except five of these children showed considerable improvement and those five did not deteriorate. The amounts gained varied considerably between individual children and the improvements were greatest in the case of the most intelligent children. Some who made little or no gain evidently needed specialist care; but the conclusion is drawn that less severely maladjusted children can be helped very considerably by interested and sympathetic teachers.

Symonds (1950) noted that though there did not seem to be any 'best' type of teaching personality, very often the teacher who succeeded did so by providing something that was missing in the child's home life. That the power to do this was the result of social proficiency rather than intelligence on the part of the teacher was suggested by Jackson (1940). As long ago as 1904 Book produced evidence of a negative kind in this connection. When a large group of boys and girls who left school early were asked why they did so, the most common reasons given were discouragement and lack of interest, but rather more than 10% mentioned specifically their dislike of particular teachers who had little sympathy with or understanding of their pupils.

How much are teachers really aware of the social conditions in their classrooms and of the significance of their own behaviour? Withall (1956) tells of observations spread over a period of twelve weeks in an eighth-grade art class. There were twenty-six children and each session was recorded on tape and by 15-second time-lapse photographs. After eleven sessions the results were analysed.

It was found that two pupils, both of whom were well-adjusted, between them were getting more than a quarter of the teacher's attention, and that eight others combined got less than these two. Among those getting little or no attention were some who were problem cases.

These results were discussed with the teacher, who was sincerely concerned about his pupils. As a result he attempted to spread his attention more evenly, but although there was some improvement there was still a lack of balance. Withall concluded that even a teacher who has a high degree of social sensitivity and who develops considerable rapport with his pupils will not necessarily distribute his attention among them as he and others would think desirable on the basis of objective evidence of their needs. For a teacher to change the pattern of his response, even when he is consciously attempting to do so, is not easy. This agrees with Symonds's (1950) observation that teachers respond in the classroom as they do out of it, in ways which have been built up over many years, and that, while their teaching techniques may be modified, their personal response to their pupils represents a deeper core of the personality which is not easily changed. This is supported by Withall's (1949) observation that, within limits, there is a constant pattern of verbal behaviour for a given teacher from day to day. There is therefore a strong case for encouraging student teachers to consider and observe their own behaviour towards their pupils before this has become too habitual to be easily changed.

If teachers are to respond successfully to the needs of their pupils, they must first of all be aware of those needs and of the characteristics and potentialities of the pupils. On the intellectual and academic side there is evidence that teachers do make accurate estimates of their pupils' abilities and attainments, and Richardson (1956) and Yates and Pidgeon (1957) have found that head teachers of primary schools can forecast satisfactorily the level of achievement likely to be reached by their pupils during their subsequent secondary school careers. It must, however, be pointed out that in making their assessments head teachers have at their disposal a considerable amount of information concerning the past school attainments of their pupils, and that their assessments cannot be considered as being entirely independent of test results. The academic progress of their pupils is usually watched keenly by teachers and it is one aspect of their behaviour which is particularly easily observed.

Other aspects of pupils' behaviour might be less open to inspection by their teachers, and it is not unlikely that teachers may make more accurate assessments of academic standing and potential than of sociometric standing, opinions and personality qualities. Indeed, Nath (1948) found that personality ratings of their pupils made by teachers were highly correlated with the results of tests in English and arithmetic. It is arguable that this is as it should be, for progress in school subjects is related not only to the ability of the pupils but also to the amount and type of effort they make, and these will depend on personality as well as intellectual qualities, but there is further evidence that teachers tend to confuse scholastic with personality qualities.

Ausubel, Schiff and Zeleny (1954) gave a battery of tests of adjustment, sociometric status and traits such as persistence, scholastic competitiveness and academic aspiration to twenty-four boys and twenty-six girls, of mean age 15·8 years and the majority of whom came from professional homes. They were also rated on these qualities by five of their current teachers.

It was found that while the teachers' ratings of adjustment and aspiration were highly reliable, they did not correlate significantly with other measures of adjustment, though they were more valid for the girls than for the boys. Teachers tended to regard as well-adjusted pupils whom they perceived as persistent and scholastically competitive, who were well-accepted by other pupils, who had good scholastic records, and whose aspirations matched their achievement. The teachers rated aspiration on the basis of the pupils' achievement. The low correlations between the teachers' ratings of their pupils' adjustment and the pupils' actual scores on such tests as the Rorschach and Minnesota Multiphasic Personality Inventory suggests that they were not measuring the same thing, and that the teachers' conception of a well-adjusted pupil might be faulty.

Factors which may affect a teacher's assessment of the sociometric status of children in a group are discussed by Bonney (1943b). Toleration, passive acceptance and kindness or sympathy shown to one child by others are often mistaken by the teacher for positive preference. There are also certain types of pupil whose sociometric status is over- or under-estimated by teachers. Four types who are apt to be over-rated by teachers are noted (Bonney, 1947).

1. Those who are courteous or responsive to the teacher, and more socially smooth and aggressive than the average, but who have unfavourable personality traits which they do not show to the teacher.
2. Those who are outstanding in one or more capacities but who are unskilled in interpersonal relations.
3. Those who have desirable personality traits which show in dealings with teachers, but who are socially inhibited with their equals.
4. Those who have desirable personality traits as above, but who are regarded as outsiders by their equals.

Two types who are often under-rated by teachers are also given.

1. Those who make a poor response to the kind of group situation they are in, who are not outstanding, but who can establish intimate relations within a small circle or with a few people outside their circle.
2. Those who antagonize the teacher, disregard regulations, or offend his moral conceptions, but who are well-liked by some of their equals.

Teachers and pupils do not always use the same standards of judgment in cases of these kinds, and so discrepancies occur between the real status of the pupils and the teachers' estimates.

That teachers and pupils do make the same judgments on occasion is shown in a study by Edwards (1952). In a boys' secondary school prefects were appointed by the headmaster. As part of a sociometric test, a mock election of prefects was held among the boys before the actual appointments were made. It was found that the headmaster and the boys independently chose the same prefects, and that only in the choice of the head boy was there a difference between them. The prefects chosen remained acceptable to the boys throughout the year and the head boy improved his status. Here headmaster and boys were choosing boys to occupy a particular position in a society they both knew well. Both chose the people who seemed most suitable, and the boys did not choose on a basis of friendship. There was a degree of objectivity here which is not found when sociometric status is under consideration, and this probably accounts for the similarity in the choice made by headmaster and boys.

Another aspect of this question concerns the awareness of teachers of the opinions held by their pupils. Goertzen (1957) obtained the opinions of 1773 seventh-grade children about a number of types of neutral and negative behaviour classed as aggressive, delinquency-related, nonconforming and withdrawing. Fifty-seven teachers and thirty-six psychologists were asked to respond to the questionnaire as they thought the children would, while another fifty-five teachers were asked to give their own opinions. High correlations (+0·90 and over) were found between the responses of the teachers and the children, whether the teachers were estimating the children's responses or giving their own. The psychologists' responses correlated +0·79 with those of the children and +0·82 with those of the teachers. This may mean that any group of people in our society would make the same judgments of these types of behaviour, but it also indicates that adults understand children's feelings about them and share them. It would be interesting to discover in what fields this is true, and whether there are any areas of thought in which the standards of adults and children differ considerably.

That teachers are not always aware of divisions between their pupils is shown by Blyth (1958). A sociometric test in a junior school brought to light a cleavage between two groups of boys of which the teachers were unaware. The groups were not in any sense hostile to one another but they did not mix. The boys in them differed in intelligence and patterns of leisure-time activity, and lived in different districts, though they were of much the same socio-economic status. If the state had been one of aggression rather than peaceful coexistence it would probably have been noted. Since it caused no trouble to anyone, it passed without notice. This is a commentary on the types of behaviour which catch the attention of teachers.

It is pertinent at this point, after considering the knowledge which teachers have of their pupils, to inquire about the qualities of those pupils whom teachers like or dislike. Gronlund (1953) obtained sociometric gradings of children in each of forty sixth-grade classes, and also asked their teachers, all women, to choose the three children they most preferred and the three they least preferred to have in their classes. It was found that approximately half the pupils most preferred by their teachers had been rated as stars, while none were isolates, though 11% were classed as neglectees. Of those least preferred by their teachers more than half were isolates or neglectees, while less than 4% were stars. Evidently the characteristics which make children acceptable or unacceptable to their peers also influence, and in the same direction, their relationships with their teachers.

An attempt to find out what qualities in the pupils contributed to poor relations between them and their teachers was made by Birchmore (1951). A list of qualities which the teachers in a boys' secondary grammar school considered affected their pleasure in teaching the boys was drawn up. The teachers also indicated the amount of pleasure they derived from teaching individual pupils, and two groups of boys, those with the highest and lowest pleasure scores, were identified for further study. It was found that staff-pupil relationships were best in those forms where the best results were obtained, and that the pleasure of the staff in teaching them was correlated more highly with the actual attainment of the boys than with the amount of effort they made. The coefficients were $+0.64$ and $+0.55$ respectively, and both were significant.

The qualities which detracted most seriously from the pleasure the staff felt in teaching the boys were those which were 'in one way or another liable to be interpreted as attacks upon the teacher or as leading to such attacks'. The boys who were disliked were described as insolent, disobedient, loutish, inattentive, lazy, feeling that the subject was useless, or refusing to think unless forced to do so. Talkativeness and surliness did not seem to matter so much, though dirtiness might do so. An interesting comment was that the pupils in this school appeared to hold more complimentary opinions of the staff's qualities than the staff held of those of the pupils.

There have been many inquiries about the qualities which pupils like in their teachers. An early one was conducted by Kratz (1896), who had noted that 'in describing that model teacher, the eminent educator draws largely from his own experience, and clothes his model with his own characteristics, supplemented, it may be, by some traits observed in other successful teachers, and rounded out by a few more, evolved from his own inner consciousness'. In an attempt at greater objectivity, Kratz asked over two thousand children of junior school age to describe the best teacher they had ever had. The qualities most frequently mentioned in the descriptions were help in studies, personal appearance and goodness or kindness.

Since the appearance of the study by Kratz (1896) there has been a spate of similar studies in which children of all ages, students and adults have been asked about the personal qualities of teachers they had liked or disliked and about the amount of good they thought they had derived from the efforts of their teachers. Mention may be made in this connection of the work of Bell (1900), Book (1905), Bird (1917), Reymert (1917), Dolch (1920), Hollis (1935), Tiedeman (1942) and Geyer (1946). The degree of unanimity among the findings of these investigators is quite remarkable, especially when one considers the variations so frequently found between the results of psychological studies of similar phenomena. Children, apparently, know quite clearly what they like and what they dislike in their teachers, and different generations of school children have held the same opinions for a period of over fifty years. They like teachers who are kind, friendly, cheerful, patient, helpful, fair, have a sense of humour, show an understanding of children's problems, allow plenty of pupil activity and at the same time maintain order. They dislike teachers who use sarcasm and ridicule, are domineering and have favourites, who punish to secure discipline, fail to provide for the needs of individual pupils, and have disagreeable personality peculiarities.

Among college students, too, there is close agreement on what qualities are most to be desired in their teachers. They are older than school children and possibly also abler than the average, and are more likely to stress the importance of the teachers' knowledge of their subject matter and their ability to teach it well. This was brought out by Geyer (1946), who found that students valued qualities concerned with the actual teaching of the course more highly than such things as sincerity, sense of humour and the appearance of their teachers. At the same time students admit that their teachers influence them in many ways, and a group questioned by Bell (1900) listed influences in moral and social spheres as well as intellectual ones. According to both Bell (1900) and Reymert (1917) the influence of the teacher seems to reach a peak during adolescence, and at a slightly earlier age among girls than among boys.

It may be asked whether we ought to place much reliance on the opinions of pupils about their teachers. Children are immature and their judgments may, as a result, be unsound. When they are older and view their teachers in retrospect they may hold very different views about them, and may reach a different assessment of the relative values of the contributions to their education made by different teachers.

Jersild (1940) obtained retrospective reports from a number of adults about the teachers they had liked and disliked at school, and compared the lists of qualities they mentioned with similar lists obtained from school children. It was found that the teachers' human qualities as people were mentioned oftener by the adults than the children, whereas the children mentioned oftener than did the adults the teachers' characteristics as disciplinarians or directors of classes, and their performances as teachers teaching. Adults, in fact, tended to judge their childhood teachers in terms of qualities which are generally considered desirable in any human beings, but the children were more concerned with their teachers specifically as teachers, the role in which they saw them daily.

In Jersild's study the adults and the children were rating different teachers, so the comparison between the two groups was restricted to a consideration of the types of qualities they thought important. Drucker and Remmers (1951) asked past and present students of Purdue University to rate the same members of the staff, whom both groups had known. Correlations between ratings made by the two groups of a number of personal qualities of the staff ranged from +0·40 to +0·68. It was found that present students tended to give higher ratings than past students on most traits, but that most of the differences were too small to be of practical significance. There was close agreement between the past and present students on the qualities desirable in college instructors, and the writers concluded that 'the judgments made by undergraduates of their instructors are valid ones in terms of permanence and maturity'.

A similar result was obtained by Boyce and Bryan (1944). Their method was to ask adults whose schooldays were at least five years back first, to recall their reactions when in class to their teachers, and then, to rate those same teachers from an adult standpoint on the benefits they believed they had received while in their classes. They found that very little change of opinion was evident, and that where there was a marked change it was sometimes the result of later contacts with the teachers.

From these studies it seems that the views of children and adults about their teachers do not differ very much, and that the opinions about teachers formed in the classroom are very likely to persist in later years. This underlines the importance of ensuring that harmonious relations between pupils and teachers shall exist, and that the utmost care be taken to choose and train teachers in such a way as to ensure that they give the best possible care to the children in their charge. As Bush (1942) has pointed out, the pupil-teacher relationship is a complex one, and its effectiveness is limited by the particular purposes of both the pupil and the teacher, by the needs of the pupil, and by the ability of the teacher to meet particular types of pupil needs.

IX

TEACHERS AND TEACHING

NO study of the classroom group would be complete without some discussion of the teacher as a person and of the work he or she does in school. Teachers and their influence on and relationship to their pupils have been considered in the last chapter, and this chapter will be devoted to other aspects of teaching.

Some inquiries have been made into the reasons given by individuals for their choice of career, both in general and with particular reference to teaching. When Vernon (1937) questioned forty-seven women university students between the ages of 20 and 25, she found a strong tendency among them to select careers in conformity with the social standards of the groups to which they belonged. If this is a general tendency, and it well may be, it seems likely that in groups where teaching enjoys high prestige many young people may be expected to choose to become teachers. Conversely, if for any reason the prestige of teaching drops, then it is likely that other careers will be chosen instead.

Support for this view is to be found in accounts of studies carried out by Austin (1931), Valentine (1934) and Tudhope (1944) in England, and Seagoe (1942) in America. The English studies were carried out at a time of economic depression, and it was very noticeable that the security of teaching in contrast to the insecurity of some other types of work increased its prestige and made it appear more desirable than it might otherwise have done. It was also a career of which parents approved, and their wishes had carried some weight in the decisions to teach taken by many of the students questioned by Valentine and Tudhope. Seagoe found that a group of students intending to teach had been significantly more often advised to do so that a similar group not intending to teach.

Economic and social reasons are obviously important but they are not the only ones that weigh in the choice of a career, and many people choose one because they think they will enjoy the work involved or the conditions under which it is carried on. It has been noted, however, that school children often have very inadequate knowledge or erroneous ideas about what is involved in different occupations, and Austin (1931) found that this was true of teaching, the most popular profession among over a thousand secondary school children questioned. Of these few gave sound reasons for their choice, and possibly many chose teaching as the only career with which they had any real familiarity. It is sometimes found that pupils who enjoy school want to become teachers, and Evans (1946) found that among sixteen-year-old grammar school pupils attitude to school was significantly correlated with attitude towards teaching as a career. The danger here is that pupils who are happy at school but who are reluctant to grow up may choose to teach because by so doing they will be able to remain in the sheltered world they know. Austin found evidence of this among the children in her sample.

A mature interest in and liking for children and the desire to help in their upbringing is quite a different type of motive. Here the teacher is prepared to play an adult role in the classroom and has no desire to remain a child among children. Both Valentine (1934) and Tudhope (1944) found that this was a frequently given reason for taking up teaching, and it may be questioned whether anyone who does not have this type of interest in teaching should ever be advised to teach.

Another common reason given was interest in a particular subject and a desire to study it to an advanced level. Although this may be a reason for enjoying a course of preparation for teaching, it may in the end be a reason for unhappiness as a teacher. In school most of a teacher's time is spent in teaching at a comparatively elementary level, well below the teacher's own level of achievement, and if interest is in the subject rather than in the children this may be frustrating. Birkinshaw (1935) found that among women teachers in grammar schools interest in study rather than in children was sometimes a cause of maladjustment.

The causes of maladjustment in teaching are many and varied, and it is important that those who are in contact with young teachers should have an adequate knowledge of them. In an inquiry into the problems of young teachers, Phillips (1932) found that breakdowns were more often the result of several causes than of one single cause. Professional difficulties, such as bad working conditions, poor discipline and unsatisfactory staff relationships, were possibly the most serious ones, but personality difficulties and social and economic problems also came into the picture.

A dislike for dealing with large groups of people was noted by Birkinshaw (1935) as a cause of unhappiness in some teachers. Champ (1948) also found it given by some women teachers as one of their reasons for withdrawal from the profession, but Evans (1952a) found no connection between the size of the group to which the teacher preferred to belong and his or her efficiency. Students who preferred to be members of small groups, or even to be solitary, were neither better nor worse teachers than those who preferred to be members of larger groups. It is suggested that this may be because the teacher in the classroom group occupies a unique position as the only adult present, and so need not feel submerged as might happen in a large adult group. There is no reason to assume that disliking being a member of a large group will, by itself, militate against success in teaching, though in combination with other factors it may do so.

Another reason for withdrawal found by Champ (1948) was weak discipline, and Birkinshaw (1935) found that unhappiness was caused by a lack of skill in imparting knowledge. Both these seem to indicate an inability to deal with large groups, and if this is the cause for disliking them then the teacher will be unsuccessful, but it should be noted that the primary reason for failure is not the dislike of large groups.

Both Birkinshaw and Champ found that some women

disliked teaching because they found it too strenuous physically or mentally, and their health suffered. Some had taken it up without any clear idea of its demands, or had believed they could overcome the difficulties. In Birkinshaw's sample, the unsuccessful teachers had not enjoyed their own schooldays as much as had the successful teachers.

It is sometimes possible to help teachers to improve their adjustment to their work and so to increase their chances of happiness in it. In one case, Wrightstone, Beaumont, Forlano and Gastwirth (1952) used sociometric methods to improve personal relationships among the members of the staffs of seven schools. Among teachers, as among their pupils, there are some who are stars and some who are isolates, and the aim was to improve the adjustment of the isolates. The method was to identify them and draw them into group activities in much the way used with pupils in a class, and the results obtained showed that the method was successful.

In another case Daldy (1937) studied the success of a group of thirty-one domestic science students in relation to their powers of adaptation. This was taken to mean the ability to adjust to a situation without undue emotional conflict or display of emotion and without inducing conflict in the environment. About half the group were noted as having difficulties of adaptation and this was reacting unfavourably on their performance as teachers. When their difficulties were discussed with them in a manner leading to emotional relief it was found that an improvement in their teaching followed.

It is worth taking some trouble to identify as early as possible those teachers who are likely to need help in adjusting to the school situation, and it is much better if this can be done during their course of training rather than later, when help may be less easily available. Cornwell (1958) has described a method he devised for picking out, near the beginning of their training, those students who were likely to fail the course, or who would need special help if they were to be successful. The criterion of success in the course included examination results, a general assessment of the student as a potential teacher, and a mark for practical teaching. This criterion was compared with the results of sociometric and near sociometric tests and a rank correlation of $+0\cdot67$ was obtained. The correlation between the sociometric tests and the final teaching mark was $+0\cdot57$. When it is realized that the sociometric tests were given during the second term and the criterion and teaching assessments made during the sixth term of the course, it seems that these results deserve serious consideration.

So far in this chapter no attempt has been made to indicate what is meant by success in teaching. Many studies have been made of the efficiency of teachers, and nearly everyone is sure that they know what is meant by good teaching until they attempt to define it. Then difficulties arise, and these are reflected in the wide variety of criteria of good teaching which have been used at one time or another. Birkinshaw (1935) has suggested that happiness in the work is the least objectionable criterion of teaching success available, since it implies that the happy teacher has 'both the affection and regard of many of those with whom and for whom she works'. It is not usual, however, to assess teacher competence in terms of happiness. Stott (1950) has given examination results, discipline, the character and personality development of pupils, and skill in handling backward or problem children as factors usually taken into account by parents.

Since teachers are concerned with producing and encouraging desirable changes in their pupils, the obvious way of assessing the effectiveness of any teacher is by measuring the changes in his or her pupils, and a suitable measure of pupil achievement has often been advocated as a measure of teaching efficiency. Unfortunately the application of this principle is anything but easy. The changes produced in children by their teachers are many and varied, including changes in knowledge, in attitudes and ideals, in purpose and in personality. It is therefore necessary to decide what changes should be taken into account.

The most obvious and easiest change to measure is the change in knowledge. Testing before and after instruction is possible, and the method has been widely used in assessing teaching efficiency. It is not a satisfactory method, since many factors besides the efficiency of the teacher contribute to a child's learning. Some of these factors were investigated by Arvidson

(1956), who found that the ability of the teacher played a relatively small part in determining the academic success of his pupils in English and arithmetic. Intelligence and home background, factors outside the teacher's range of influence, appeared to be the most important determiners of success.

When we come to consider other changes we are on even more debatable ground. Behaviour, attitudes and ideals are not easily measured, and changes in them over a period cannot usually be assigned with certainty to the influence of a particular teacher, or indeed to any one cause. In view of these considerations pupil change cannot, by itself, be taken as a satisfactory measure of teacher efficiency.

A more generally used criterion is based upon the judgment of experts who are familar with the work of the teacher and have observed him or her in the classroom. This is probably the easiest method of assessing teaching efficiency at present available, and it depends on the assumption that it is possible for school principals, supervisors and other educational experts to recognize good teaching when they see it, and to assess the efficiency of one teacher in relation to that of others. Sandiford (1937) considered this to be the only valid criterion available.

The main objection to this method is that it uses a subjective assessment, depending on the impression made on the assessor. Knight (1923), Odenweller (1936), Brown (1938) and Jayne (1945) have all presented evidence of differences in assessments made by different assessors. Many causes for these differences have been suggested. The most obvious is that the assessors are not all taking into account the same aspects of a teacher's performance or are attaching different degrees of importance to them.

One method of overcoming this difficulty is by the use of rating scales. These consist of lists of qualities which their authors consider to be necessary in a teacher. Many people have drawn up lists of qualities which should be considered in judging teachers, and lists by Thomson (1921), Charters and Waples (1929) and Cattell (1931) may be cited as examples both of types of such lists and of modes of preparation. In considering any such list it is pertinent to inquire who drew it up and on what grounds the various qualities were included.

In many cases these lists appear to express little except the opinions of their authors. This seems to be true of the lists drawn up by Witham (1914), Sprague (1917), Connor (1920), Kent (1920), Thomson (1921) and Freyd (1923). In other lists, such as those drawn up by Charters and Waples (1929), Cattell (1931) and Bryan (1937), the qualities to be rated represent a consensus of opinion as to the qualities desirable in teachers. The qualities found in these lists are very varied, but they generally include such things as physical characteristics, speech, intelligence, scholarship and attitudes.

Although the use of such a scale does not increase the objectivity of ratings, it does help to ensure that all assessors take into account the same aspects of a teacher's work and personality, and that no important aspects are completely overlooked. The substitution of a number of subjective judgments for one comprehensive one does not, however, necessarily improve the final rating. Hampton (1951) found that trait ratings of teachers were highly correlated with general category ratings, and concluded that individual trait ratings add little to our knowledge but may be useful for diagnostic purposes.

One of the difficulties in rating teachers is the fact that there are not usually many people who are sufficiently familiar with their work to rate them accurately. The people who see most of their teachers' work are the pupils, and some investigators have used ratings made by pupils as a criterion of teaching efficiency. Bryan (1937) claimed that such ratings, in so far as they measure the pupils' opinions of their teachers, are, of necessity, valid. Whether they are valid measures of teaching efficiency is another matter. Evidence that pupil ratings are highly reliable produced by Bryan (1937), Heilman and Armentrout (1936) and Cook and Leeds (1947), and factors influencing pupils' ratings of their teachers have already been discussed.

A number of studies have included the correlation of different measures of teaching efficiency. In the main the correlation coefficients reported have been low. This is true in the studies by Crabbs (1925), Bryan (1937), Jayne (1945), Brookover (1945) and Cook and Leeds (1947). Knight (1922) reported satisfactory agreement between ratings made by supervisors

I   121

and pupils. Shannon (1936) produced correlations ranging from 0·29 to 0·97 between score card scores and general informal estimates of teaching efficiency. Porter (1942) found close agreement between ratings made by supervisors and pupils of the best and poorest teachers, but greater divergence in the case of the middle group.

As well as considering the possibility that different methods of assessing teaching efficiency are not all measuring the same variable, it must be borne in mind that the performance of any one teacher is not necessarily uniform. Lancelot (1935) studied a group of teachers of mathematics and found that the effectiveness of their teaching varied according to the level of ability of their pupils and the branch of the subject being taught. Crabbs (1925) had earlier obtained a similar result.

Variations in a teacher's performance over a period of time may also be expected, as is evidenced by a number of studies in which students' practice teaching marks are compared with assessments of their work made later in their careers. The impression left by such studies as those of Seagoe (1946), Odenweller (1936), Sandiford (1937), Lins (1946) and Jones (1946) in America, and Tudhope (1942 and 1943), Walters (1957) and Collins (1959) in Britain is that although practice teaching marks are some indication of future teaching success, the circumstances in which the teacher has to work may cause considerable fluctuations in teaching efficiency.

There have been a great many studies in which assessments of teaching efficiency have been correlated with assessments of other qualities of the teacher. The main qualities considered in this way can be classified as physical characteristics, intelligence, scholarship, professional information, attitudes and interests, and personality. Usually the resulting correlations have been low and often they have been insignificant, though exceptions exist, as in the work of Panton (1934) and Lovell (1951), where the two sets of assessments were made by the same people. Appreciable correlations obtained in this way are as likely to be evidence of halo as of any true relationship between the qualities considered and teaching efficiency. Where the assessments of teaching efficiency are made by one group and those of other qualities by another group, as in the study reported by Uttley (1952), fewer significant correlations are likely to be found. The same is true when assessments of teaching efficiency are compared with the results of psychological or other tests, as was done by Evans (1952a), Phillips (1953) and Walters (1957). In fairness it must be mentioned that in all these cases the results relate to selected groups, and it is well known that where the range of scores is restricted by selection correlations are artificially depressed. Groups of students are relatively homogeneous in ability and possibly in some other qualities, and it is likely that correlations obtained from them are lower than the true level for the general population or even for an unselected group of applicants for training as teachers.

Of recent years, as a result of the application of factor analysis to sets of correlation coefficients between teaching efficiency and other qualities of the teacher, a number of investigators have produced evidence of qualities which contribute to success in teaching. It is noticeable that these studies, instead of resulting in long lists of more or less independent personality traits, tend to produce evidence of the importance of a few much more general characteristics.

Smalzried and Remmers (1943) factor analysed the results of the Purdue Rating Scale for Instructors from forty practice teachers. They found that two factors were sufficient to account for the table of intercorrelations. These were an empathy trait, described as 'the ability to wear each students "sensorial and emotional" shoes', and a professional maturity trait.

Hellfritzch (1945) applied factor analysis to the results of a large number of measures of teaching ability given to two groups of twenty-eight and fifty-seven teachers. He found that four common factors were sufficient to account for the interrelationship of the nineteen teacher abilities studied. These factors he called:

1. General knowledge and mental ability.
2. A teacher rating scale factor.
3. Personal, emotional and social adjustment.
4. Eulogizing attitude towards the teaching profession.

He concluded, however, that 'no single teacher measure can

be reliably substituted for the actual measurement of pupil growth in evaluating the ability of the teacher to teach'.

Skinner (1949), dealing with teachers of technical subjects, postulated that in any teaching situation there are three focal points, the teacher, the pupils, and the material arising during the activity. Using factorial analysis, he concluded that the ability to stimulate and arouse interest, the ability to evoke pupil co-operation, and the ability to make the lesson material of value to the pupils, were the most important qualities contributing to teaching ability.

Lovell (1951) obtained ratings of a large number of emergency training college students on twelve traits. In all cases correlations between these ratings and teaching marks were significant and positive. As a result of factor analysis he found that three factors accounted for 65·8% of the variance. These factors he called:

1. Intelligence and the willingness to use it in the education of children. (57·1% of variance.)
2. An empathy factor, the ability to appear live and interesting to children. (5·6% of variance.)
3. A speech factor. (3·1% of variance.)

Ryans (1951), in a study of 275 women teachers, found five factors which accounted for teaching effectiveness.

A referred to pupil participation and openmindedness (originality, adaptability and tolerance) on the part of the teacher.
B referred to controlled pupil activity and a business-like approach on the part of the teacher.
C described the teacher who was liked by others for 'human traits' such as understanding and impartiality, and who tended to be calm and consistent.
D referred to teacher sociability (in a social environment of eight-to ten-year-old children).
E referred to the superficial appearance or attractiveness of the teacher.

Another comparatively recent development in the field of teacher-study has been reported by Domas (1950) on behalf of the New England School Development Council, and by Barr and others (1952) and Ryans and Wandt (1952a) for the

Teacher Characteristics Study of the American Council on Education. The technique consists in the collection and analysis of reports of actual incidents in which teachers showed outstandingly effective or ineffective behaviour. This is described as the Critical Incident Technique. Reports of the analysis of such data have been published by Ryans (1952), Ryans and Wandt (1952b) and Jensen (1951). The methods used by all these investigators are similar, and only the study by Jensen will be described here.

Jensen (1951) drew up a list of critical requirements for teachers after studying descriptions of 500 critical incidents in the behaviour of effective and ineffective teachers, supplied by 154 observers. A critical requirement was defined as 'any observable teacher behaviour or activity that makes the difference between success and failure in teaching'. The critical requirements are listed under three main headings.

1. *Personal qualities.*
   Optimism, fairness, self-control.
2. *Professional qualities.*
   Knowledge of subject matter and techniques of teaching, ability to get student response, business-like approach.
3. *Social qualities.*
   Sympathy and understanding, democracy, friendly and commending attitude, ability to judge reactions of others.

It remains to be seen how much this method will add to our knowledge of factors contributing to efficiency in teaching.

On the results obtained from the studies available, it would be difficult to point to any one quality or group of qualities which could be considered indispensable in a teacher. Probably it is safe to say that anyone whose physical and mental health is good enough to stand up to the strains of the classroom, whose intelligence and knowledge of subject matter is adequate, and who is interested in children and really wants to teach them, will have a good chance of becoming a successful teacher. This is not merely of academic interest, but is of practical importance to those who have to advise or select candidates for training as teachers, and much of the work which has been done on teaching efficiency and associated qualities has been done with a view to improving methods of selection. These are usually based on a consideration of the academic records of the candidates, reports from their head teachers, interview impressions, and sometimes psychological tests. Burroughs (1951 and 1958) reported that for all practical purposes tests, reports and interviews were unrelated and supplied different evidence about the candidates, and that, within its own limitations, the interview was as good a predictor of success as most other measures. There is scope for research in this field, and it would be useful to have a great deal more information than is available about the relationship between the results of selection procedures and the subsequent college careers of student teachers.

It is noticeable that different training colleges tend to have different types of students, and Evans (1952a) has produced evidence that there are significant differences in the results of intelligence and personality tests obtained both from different colleges and different groups within the same college. Colleges do not all offer the same training facilities, and it is to be expected that they will select from among the applicants for admission those who appear to be most likely to fit into their pattern and to benefit from the training available. This is a sound principle.

In schools, too, there is room for many different kinds of teacher, and success is often a matter of finding the right niche. We know too little about the characteristics of teachers likely to be successful in particular schools, with particular age-groups and levels of ability, and in teaching particular subjects, and research directed to providing such information is needed. It might well be more fruitful than more general studies of teaching efficiency. In the meantime, it is probably safe to agree with Birkinshaw (1935) and to conclude that happiness in the work is a good indication of success in teaching, and to add that a happy and contented classroom group is a sure sign of the influence of a good teacher.

BIBLIOGRAPHY

Page references to the present text are given in bold figures

AMATORA, M. (1955): 'Validity in self evaluation.' *Educ. and Psychol. Meas.*, 15, 119-26. **97**

ANDERSON, H. H. *et al.* (1945, 1946, 1946): *Studies of Teachers' Classroom Personalities, I, II, III.* Applied Psychology Monographs of the American Psychological Association. Stanford University Press. **102**

ARSENIAN, S. (1942): 'Own estimate and objective measurement.' *J. Educ. Psychol.*, 33, 291-302. **94**

ARVIDSON, G. L. (1956): *Some Factors Influencing the Achievement of First Year Secondary Modern School Children.* Unpublished Ph.D. Thesis, University of London Library. **105**

AUSTIN, F. M. (1931): 'An analysis of the motives of adolescents for the choice of the teaching profession.' *Brit. J. Educ. Psychol.*, 1, 87-103. **115, 116**

AUSUBEL, D. P. (1953): 'Reciprocity and assumed reciprocity of acceptance among adolescents, a sociometric study.' *Sociometry*, 16, 339-48. **95**

— (1955): 'Sociempathy as a function of sociometric status in an adolescent group.' *Human Relations*, 8, 75-84. **90, 95**

— SCHIFF, H. M. and ZELENY, M. P. (1954): 'Validity of teachers' ratings of adolescents' adjustment and aspirations.' *J. Educ. Psychol.*, 45, 394-406. **108**

BARKER, P. G. (1942): 'The social interrelations of strangers and acquaintances.' *Sociometry*, 5, 169-79. **13, 44, 85**

BARON, D. (1951): 'Personal-social characteristics and classroom social status: A sociometric study of fifth and sixth grade girls.' *Sociometry*, 14, 32-42. **91**

BARR, A. S. *et al.* (1952): 'Report of a committee on the criteria of teacher effectiveness.' *Rev. Educ. Res.*, 22, 238-63. **124**

BARTLETT, C. J. (1960): 'Dimensions of leadership behavior in classroom discussion groups.' *J. Educ. Psychol.*, 50, 280-4.

BASSETT, R. E. (1944): 'Cliques in a student body of stable membership.' *Sociometry*, 7, 290-302. **70**

BAXTER, B. (1950): *Teacher-Pupil Relationships*. New York: Macmillan Company.

BECKER, M. G. and LOOMIS, C. P. (1948): 'Measuring rural urban and farm and non-farm cleavages in a rural consolidated school.' *Sociometry*, 11, 246-61. **46, 72, 73**

BEDOIAN, V. H. (1953): 'Mental health analysis of socially over-accepted, socially under-accepted, overage and underage pupils in the sixth grade.' *J. Educ. Psychol.*, 44, 366-71. **92**

BELL, S. (1900): 'A study of the teacher's influence.' *Ped. Sem.*, 7, 492-525. **112, 113**

BERKOWITZ, L. (1954): 'Group standards, cohesiveness and productivity.' *Human Relations*, 7, 509-19. **73**

BEUM, C. O. and BRUNDAGE, E. G. (1950): 'A method for analyzing the sociomatrix.' *Sociometry*, 13, 141-5. **27**

BEVERSTOCK, A. G. (1949): 'Group methods applied to youth leader selection.' *Brit. J. Educ. Psychol.*, 19, 112-20.

BIRCHMORE, B. (1951): *A Study of the Relationships between Pupils and Teachers in Certain Classes in a Secondary Modern School*. Unpublished M.A. Thesis, University of London Library. **111**

BIRD, G. E. (1917): 'Pupils' estimates of teachers.' *J. Educ. Psychol.*, 8, 35-40. **112**

BIRKINSHAW, M. (1935): *The Successful Teacher*. London: Hogarth Press. **117, 119, 126**

BLUE, J. T. (1958): 'The effect of group study on grade achievement.' *J. Educ. Psychol.*, 49, 118-23. **75**

BLUM, M. L. (1936): 'An investigation of the relation existing between students' grades and their ratings of the instructor's ability to teach.' *J. Educ. Psychol.*, 27, 217-21. **99**

BLYTH, W. A. L. (1958): 'Sociometry, prefects and peaceful coexistence in a junior school.' *Soc. Rev.*, 6, 5-24. **71, 110**

— (1960): 'The sociometric study of children's groups in English schools.' *Brit. J. Educ. Stud.*, 8, 127-47. **7**

BOARDMAN, C. W. (1928) *Professional Tests as Measures of Teaching Efficiency in High School*. New York: Teachers College, Columbia University. **99**

BOGARDUS, E. S. (1934): *Leaders and Leadership*. New York: D. Appleton Century. **58**

Bibliography

BONNEY, M. E. (1943a): 'Values of sociometric studies in the classroom.' *Sociometry*, 6, 251-4. **45, 46, 53, 54**

— (1943b): 'The constancy of sociometric scores and their relationship to teacher judgments of social success, and to personality self-ratings.' *Sociometry*, 6, 409-24. **41, 53, 55, 108**

— (1943c): 'Personality traits of socially successful and socially unsuccessful children.' *J. Educ. Psychol.*, 34, 499-72.

— (1946): 'A sociometric study of the relationship of some factors to mutual friendships on the elementary, secondary and college levels.' *Sociometry*, 9, 21-47.

— (1947): 'Sociometric study of agreement between teacher judgments and student choices.' *Sociometry*, 10, 133-46. **109**

— (1955): 'A study of constancy of sociometric ranks among college students over a two-year period.' *Sociometry*, 18, 531-42. **42, 45**

BOOK, W. F. (1904): 'Why pupils drop out of high school.' *Ped. Sem.*, 11, 204-32. **106**

— (1905): 'The high school teacher from the pupil's point of view.' *Ped. Sem.*, 12, 239-88. **112**

BORGATTA, E. F. (1951): 'A diagnostic note on the construction of sociograms and action diagrams.' *Group Psychotherapy*, 3, 300-8. **12, 13, 21**

BOYCE, R. B. and BRYAN, R. C. (1944): 'To what extent do pupils' opinions of teachers change in later years?' *J. Educ. Res.*, 37, 698-705. **114**

BRADBURN, E. (1954): *Social Relationships of Children in Infant Schools Using Different Teaching Methods*. Unpublished M.Ed. Thesis, University of Manchester Library. **77**

BRETSCH, H. S. (1952): 'Social skills and activities of socially accepted and unaccepted adolescents.' *J. Educ. Psychol.*, 43, 449-58. **93**

BRONFENBRENNER, U. (1943): 'A constant frame of reference for sociometric research.' *Sociometry*, 6, 363-97.

— (1944): 'The graphic presentation of sociometric data.' *Sociometry*, 7, 283-9. **22**

— (1945): *The Measurement of Sociometric Status, Structure and Development*. Sociometry Monographs No. 6. New York: Beacon House. **24, 33**

BROOKOVER, W. B. (1940): 'Person-person interaction between teachers and pupils and teaching effectiveness.' *J. Educ. Res.*, 34, 272-87.

— (1945): 'The relation of social factors to teaching ability.' *J. Exp. Educ.*, 13, 191-205. **99, 100, 121**

Bibliography

BROWN, E. E. (1938): *The Selection and Education of Oklahoma High School Teachers*. Oklahoma: Harlow Publishing Co. **120**

BROWNFAIN, J. J. (1952): 'Stability of the self-concept as a dimension of personality.' *J. Abn. and Soc. Psychol.*, 47, 597-606. **89**

BRYAN, R. C. (1937): *Pupil Rating of Secondary School Teachers*. New York: Teachers College, Columbia University. **98, 99, 100, 121**

BUCHHEIMER, A. and PENDLETON, P. (1954): 'The reliability and validity of the Group Participation Scale.' *Educ. and Psychol. Meas.*, 14, 566-9. **97**

BURROUGHS, G. E. R. (1951): *Selection of Students for Training as Teachers*. Unpublished Ph.D. Thesis, University of Birmingham Library. **126**

— (1958): 'A study of the interview in the selection of students for teacher training.' *Brit. J. Educ. Psychol*, 28, 37-46. **126**

BUSH, R. N. (1942): 'A study of student-teacher relationships.' *J. Educ. Res.*, 35, 645-56. **114**

BYRD, E. (1951): 'A study of validity and constancy of choices in a sociometric test.' *Sociometry*, 14, 175-81.

CATTELL, R. B. (1931): 'The assessment of teaching ability.' *Brit. J. Educ. Psychol.*, 1, 48-72. **120, 121**

— and STICE, G. F. (1954): 'Four formulae for selecting leaders on the basis of personality.' *Human Relations*, 7, 493-507. **59**

CHABOT, J. (1950): 'A simplified example of the use of matrix multiplication for the analysis of sociometric data.' *Sociometry*, 13, 131-40. **39**

CHAMP, J. M. (1948): *A Study of the Attitude of Women Students, Teachers and Former Teachers towards Teaching as a Career*. Unpublished M.A. Thesis, University of London Library. **117**

CHAPIN, F. S. (1940): 'Trends in sociometrics and critique.' *Sociometry*, 3, 245-62. **10**

CHARTERS, W. W. and WAPLES, D. (1929): *The Commonwealth Teacher-Training Study*. Chicago: University of Chicago Press. **120, 121**

CHOWDHRY, K. and NEWCOMB, T. M. (1952): 'The relative abilities of leaders and non-leaders to estimate opinions of their own groups.' *J. Abn. and Soc. Psychol.*, 47, 51-7. **63**

COGAN, M. L. (1958): 'The behavior of teachers and the productive behavior of their pupils.' *J. Educ. Psychol.*, 27, 89-124.

COHEN, A. R. (1958): 'Upward communication in experimentally created hierarchies.' *Human Relations*, 11, 41-53. **69**

COLLINS, M. (1959): 'A follow-up study of some former graduate student teachers.' *Brit. J. Educ. Psychol.*, 29, 187-97. **122**

CONNOR, W. L. (1920): 'A new method of rating teachers.' *J. Educ. Res.*, 1, 338-58. **121**

COOK, W. W. and LEEDS, C. H. (1947): 'Measuring the teaching personality.' *Educ. and Psychol. Meas.*, 7, 399-410. **98, 100, 121**

CORNWELL, J. (1958): *Sociometric Analysis in a Residential Training College*. Unpublished Ph.D. Thesis, University of London Library. **14, 15, 118**

CRABBS, L. M. (1925): *Measuring Efficiency in Supervision and Teaching*. New York: Teachers College, Columbia University. **121**

CRISWELL, J. H. (1942): 'The saturation point as a sociometric concept.' *Sociometry*, 5, 146-50. **73**

— (1943): 'Sociometric methods of measuring group preferences.' *Sociometry*, 6, 398-408. **37**

— (1944): 'Sociometric measurement and chance.' *Sociometry*, 7, 415-21. **37**

— (1946a): 'Foundations of sociometric measurement.' *Sociometry*, 9, 7-13. **30**

— (1946b): 'Measurement of reciprocation under multiple criteria of choice.' *Sociometry*, 9, 126-7. **36**

CROFT, I. J. and GRYGIER, T. G. (1956): 'Social relationships of truants and juvenile delinquents.' *Human Relations*, 9, 439-66. **33, 48, 54**

DALDY, D. M. (1937): 'A study of adaptability in a group of teachers.' *Brit. J. Educ. Psychol.*, 7, 1-22. **118**

DANG, S. D. (1949): *A Study of Cooperation in Certain Secondary Schools*. Unpublished M.A. Thesis, University of London Library.

DEUTSCH, M. (1949): 'An experimental study of the effects of co-operation and competition upon group process.' *Human Relations*, 2, 199-231. **76, 78**

DOLCH, E. W. (1920): 'Pupils' judgments of their teachers.' *Ped. Sem.*, 27, 195-9. **112**

DOMAS, S. J. (1950): *Report of an Exploratory Study of Teacher Competence*. Cambridge, Mass.: New England School Development Council. **124**

DRUCKER, A. J. and REMMERS, H. H. (1951): 'Do alumni and students differ in their attitudes towards instructors?' *J. Educ. Psychol.*, 129-43. **113**

EDWARDS, D. S. (1948): 'The constant frame of reference problem in sociometry.' *Sociometry*, 11, 372-9. **10**

EDWARDS, T. L. (1952): *A Study of the Social Relationships of a Group of School Prefects among Themselves and with Other Members of the School Community*. Unpublished M.A. Thesis, University of London Library. **63, 65, 66, 109**

ENG, E. and FRENCH, R. L. (1948): 'The determination of sociometric status.' *Sociometry*, 11, 368-71. **31**

Bibliography

ENGLISH, O. S. and PEARSON, G. H. J. (1947): *Emotional Problems of Living*. London: Allen & Unwin. 101

EVANS, K. M. (1946): *A Study of Attitude towards Teaching as a Career*. Unpublished M.A. Thesis, University of London Library. 116

— (1951): 'A critical survey of methods of assessing teaching ability.' *Brit. J. Educ. Psychol.*, 21, 89-95. 105

— (1952a): *A Study of Teaching Ability at the Training College Stage in Relation to the Personality and Attitudes of the Student*. Unpublished Ph.D. Thesis, University of London Library. 55, 96, 117, 123, 126

— (1952b): 'A study of attitude towards teaching as a career.' *Brit. J. Educ. Psychol.*, 22, 63-70.

— (1953): 'A further study of attitude towards teaching as a career.' *Brit. J. Educ. Psychol.*, 23, 58-63.

— (1957): 'Is the concept of "interest" of significance to success in a teacher training course?' *Educ. Rev.*, 9, 205-11.

— (1958): 'An examination of the Minnesota Teacher Attitude Inventory.' *Brit. J. Educ. Psychol.*, 28, 253-7.

— (1959a): 'Research on teaching ability.' *Educ. Res.*, 1, 22-36.

— (1959b): 'The teacher-pupil relationship.' *Educ. Res.*, 2, 3-8.

EVANS, M. C. and WILSON, M. (1949): 'Friendship choices of university women students.' *Educ. and Psychol. Meas.*, 9, 307-12. 3, 50

FAUNCE, D. and BEEGLE, J. A. (1948): 'Cleavages in a relatively homogeneous group of rural youth.' *Sociometry*, 11, 207-16. 70

FAY, P. J. (1933): 'The effect of knowledge of grades on the subsequent achievement of college students.' *Psych. Bull.*, 30, 710.

FERGUSON, L. W. (1944): 'An analysis of the generality of suggestibility to group opinion.' *Char. and Pers.*, 12, 236-43.

FESTINGER, L. (1949): 'The analysis of sociograms using matrix algebra.' *Human Relations*, 2, 153-8. 38

— CARTWRIGHT, D., BARBER, K., FLEISCH, J., GOTTSDANKER, J., KEYSEN, A. and LEAVITT, G. (1947): 'A study of rumor; Its origin and spread.' *Human Relations*, 1, 464-86. 69

— TORREY, J. and WILLERMAN, B. (1954): 'Self-evaluation as a function of attraction to the group.' *Human Relations*, 7, 161-74. 7, 91

FIEDLER, F. E., WARRINGTON, W. G. and BLAISDELL, F. J. (1952): 'Unconscious attitudes as correlates of sociometric choice in a social group.' *J. Abn. and Soc. Psychol.*, 47, 790-6. 89

FIGUEROA, J. J. (1955): 'Teaching and education: The teacher and the pupil.' *Brit. J. Educ. Stud.*, 4, 24-31. 101

FLANDERS, N. A. (1951): 'Personal-social anxiety as a factor in experimental learning situations.' *J. Educ. Res.*, 45, 100-10.

FLEMING, C. M. (1948): *Adolescence: Its Social Psychology*. London: Routledge & Kegan Paul.

— (Ed.) (1951): *Studies in the Social Psychology of Adolescence*. London: Routledge & Kegan Paul.

— (1955): 'The child within the group: The bearings of field theory and sociometry on children's classroom behaviour', in *University of London Institute of Education Studies in Education No. 7*. London : Evans.

— (1958): *Teaching: A Pyschological Analysis*. London: Methuen.

FLORY, C. D., ALDEN, E. and SIMMONS, M. (1944): 'Classroom teachers improve the personality adjustment of their pupils.' *J. Educ. Res.*, 38, 1-8. **105**

FORLANO, G. and WRIGHTSTONE, J. W. (1955): 'Measuring the quality of social acceptability within a class.' *Educ. and Psychol. Meas.*, 15, 127-36.

FORRESTER, J. F. (1951): 'The attitudes of adolescents towards their own development', in C. M. Fleming (Ed.) (1951). **94**

FORSYTH, E. and KATZ, L. (1946): 'A matrix approach to the analysis of sociometric data: Preliminary report.' *Sociometry*, 9, 340-7. **24, 28**

FRANKEL, E. B. (1946): 'The social relationships of nursery school children.' *Sociometry*, 9, 200-25. **33, 41, 43**

— and POTASHIN, R. (1944): 'A survey of sociometric and pre-sociometric literature on friendship and social acceptance among children.' *Sociometry*, 7, 422-31. **50**

FRENCH, J. R. P. (1944): 'Organized and unorganized groups under fear and frustration.' *University of Iowa: Studies in Child Welfare*, 20, 231-308. **81, 82**

FRENCH, R. L. and MENSH, I. N. (1948): 'Some relationships between interpersonal judgments and sociometric status in a college group.' *Sociometry*, 11, 335-46. **71, 91**

FREYD, M. (1923): 'A graphic rating scale for teachers.' *J. Educ. Res.*, 8, 433-9. **86, 121**

— (1933): 'The graphic rating scale.' *J. Educ. Psychol.*, 14, 83-102.

FURFEY, P. H. (1926): 'An improved rating scale technique.' *J. Educ. Psychol.*, 17, 45-8. **86**

GAGE, N. L. (1953): 'Explorations in the understanding of others.' *Educ. and Psychol. Meas.*, 13, 14-26.

— and SUCI, G. (1951): 'Social perceptions and teacher-pupil relationships.' *J. Educ. Psychol.*, 42, 144-52.

GARDNER, D. E. M. (1942): *Testing Results in the Infant School*. London: Methuen. **77**

— (1950): *Long Term Results of Infant School Methods*. London: Methuen. **77**

GARDNER, G. (1956): 'Functional leadership and popularity in small groups.' *Human Relations*, 9, 491-509. **59**

GEYER, D. L. (1946): 'Qualities desired in college instructors.' *School and Society*, 63, 270-1. **112**

GIBB, C. A. (1947): 'The principles and traits of leadership.' *J. Abn. and Soc. Psychol.*, 42, 267-84. **60**

— (1951): 'An experimental approach to the study of leadership.' *Occupational Psychology*, 25, 233-48. **60**

— (1954): 'Leadership', in Lindzey, G. (Ed.) (1954).

GIDDENS, A. (1960): 'Aspects of the social structure of a university hall of residence.' *Soc. Rev.*, 8, 97-108. **3**

GILCHRIST, J. (1952): 'The formation of social groups under conditions of success and failure.' *J. Abn. and Soc. Psychol.*, 47, 174-87. **79**

GOERTZEN, S. M. (1957): 'A study of teachers' and psychologists' ability to predict seventh graders' opinions of certain behaviors of their peer group.' *J. Educ. Psychol.*, 48, 166-70. **110**

GRONLUND, N. E. (1953): 'Relationships between the sociometric status of pupils and teachers' preferences for or against having them in class.' *Sociometry*, 16, 142-50. **110**

— (1955): 'The relative stability of classroom social status with unweighted and weighted sociometric choices.' *J. Educ. Psychol.*, 46, 345-54. **32, 33**

— (1956): 'The general ability to judge sociometric status: Elementary student teachers' sociometric perceptions of classmates and pupils.' *J. Educ. Psychol.*, 47, 147-57. **96**

— (1959): *Sociometry in the Classroom*. New York: Harper. **52**

GROSSMAN, B. and WRIGHTER, J. (1948): 'The relationship between selection-rejection and intelligence, social status, and personality amongst sixth grade children.' *Sociometry*, 11, 346-55. **45, 46, 47, 91**

GUSTAD, J. W. (1952): 'Factors associated with social behaviour and adjustment: A review of the literature.' *Educ. and Psychol. Meas.*, 12, 3-19. **43, 46, 48**

HAIGH, G. V. and SCHMIDT, W. (1956): 'The learning of subject matter in teacher-centered and group-centered classes.' *J. Educ. Psychol.*, 47, 295-301. **75, 77**

HALL, C. S. and LINDZEY, G. (1957): *Theories of Personality*. New York: John Wiley. London: Chapman & Hall. **88**

HALLWORTH, H. J. (1952): *A Study of Group Relationships among Grammar School Boys and Girls between the Ages of Eleven and Sixteen Years*. Unpublished M.A. Thesis, University of London Library. **4, 48, 62, 65, 75**

Bibliography

HALLWORTH, H. J. (1957): 'Group discussion in its relevance to teacher-training.' *Educ. Rev.* 10, 41-53. **82**

HALMOS, P. (1950): 'Social isolation and anxiety.' J. of S.W. Essex Technical College and School of Art, Walthamstow, London, E.17, June, 1950. **80**

HAMBLIN, R. L. (1958): 'Group integration during a crisis.' *Human Relations*, 11, 67-76. **80, 81**

HAMPTON, N. D. (1951): 'An analysis of supervisory ratings of elementary teachers graduated from Iowa State College.' *J. Exp. Educ.*, 20, 179-216. **121**

HARRIS, H. (1949): *The Group Approach to Leadership Testing.* London: Routledge & Kegan Paul.

HAYTHORN, W., COUCH, A., HAEFNER, D., LANGHAM, P. and CARTER, L. F. (1956): 'The behavior of authoritarian and equalitarian personalities in groups.' *Human Relations*, 9, 57-74. **60**

HEBER, R. F. (1956): 'The relation of intelligence and physical maturity to social status of children.' *J. Educ. Psychol.*, 47, 158-62. **43, 45**

HEILMAN, J. D. and ARMENTROUT, W. D. (1936): 'The rating of college teachers on ten traits by their students.' *J. Educ. Psychol.*, 27, 197-216. **98, 121**

HELLFRITZCH, A. G. (1945): 'A factor analysis of teacher activities.' *J. Exp. Educ.*, 14, 166-99. **123**

HERDA, F. J. (1935): 'Some aspects of the relative instructional efficiency of men and women teachers.' *J. Educ. Res.*, 29, 196-203. **99**

HIGGINBOTHAM, P. J. (1951): 'Leaderless discussions by groups of adolescents', in Fleming, C. M. (Ed.) (1951).

HOLLIS, A. W. (1935): *The Personal Relationship in Teaching.* Unpublished M.A. Thesis, University of Birmingham Library. **112**

HOMANS, G. C. (1951): *The Human Group.* London: Routledge & Kegan Paul.

HOWELL, C. E. (1942): 'Measurement of leadership.' *Sociometry*, 5, 163-8. **60**

JACKSON, P. W. and GETZELS, J. W. (1959): 'Psychological health and classroom functioning: A study of dissatisfaction with school among adolescents.' *J. Educ. Psychol.*, 50, 295-300.

JACKSON, V. D. (1940): 'The measurement of social proficiency.' *J. Exp. Educ.*, 8, 422-74. **106**

JAYNE, C. D. (1945): 'A study of the relationship between teaching procedures and educational outcomes.' *J. Exp. Educ.*, 14, 101-134. **120, 121**

135

JENKINS, G. G. (1931): 'Factors involved in children's friendships.' *J. Educ. Psychol.*, 22, 440-8. **50**

JENNINGS, H. H. (1937): 'Structure of leadership: Development and sphere of influence.' *Sociometry*, 1, 99-143. **58**

— (1943 and 1950): *Leadership and Isolation*. Toronto: Longmans Green. **33, 53, 62**

— (1947): 'Leadership and sociometric choice', in Newcomb, T. M. and Hartley, E. L., *et al*. (1947): *Readings in Social Psychology*. New York: Henry Holt.

JENSEN, A. C. (1951): 'Determining critical requirements for teachers.' *J. Exp. Educ.*, 20, 79-85. **125**

JERSILD, A. T. (1940): 'Characteristics of teachers who are "liked best" and "disliked most".' *J. Exp. Educ.*, 9, 139-51. **112**

JOHNSON, D. G. (1953): 'Effect of vocational counseling on self-knowledge.' *Educ. and Psychol. Meas.*, 13, 330-8. **94**

JONES, R. D. (1946): 'The prediction of teaching efficiency from objective measures.' *J. Exp. Educ.*, 15, 85-99. **122**

JUOLA, A. E. (1957): 'Leaderless group discussion ratings: What do they measure?' *Educ. and Psychol. Meas.*, 17, 499-509. **63**

KATZ, L. (1953): 'A new status index derived from sociometric analysis.' *Psychometrika*, 18, 39-43. **34**

— and POWELL, J. H. (1953): 'A proposed index of the conformity of one sociometric measurement to another.' *Psychometrika*, 18, 249-6. **39**

KENT, R. A. (1920): 'What should teacher-rating scales seek to measure?' *J. Educ. Res.*, 2, 802-7. **121**

KERSTETTER, L. M. (1940): 'Re-assignment therapy in the classroom.' *Sociometry*, 3, 293-306. **3, 49, 71**

KERSTETTER, L. (1946): 'Exploring the environment in a classroom situation.' *Sociometry*, 9, 149-50. **42**

KIDD, J. W. (1951): 'An analysis of social rejection in a college men's hall of residence.' *Sociometry*, 14, 226-34. **53**

KLEIN, J. (1956): *The Study of Groups*. London: Routledge & Kegan Paul.

KNIGHT, F. B. (1922): 'Qualities related to success in elementary school teaching.' *J. Educ. Res.*, 5, 207-16. **121**

— (1923): 'The effect of the "acquaintance factor" upon personal judgments.' *J. Educ. Psychol.*, 14, 129-42. **120**

KRATZ, H. E. (1896): 'Characteristics of the teacher as recognized by children.' *Ped. Sem.*, 3, 413-18. **111, 112**

KUHLEN, R. G. and BRETSCH, H. S. (1947): 'Sociometric status and personal problems of adolescents.' *Sociometry*, 10, 122-32. **47, 53, 92**

Bibliography

KUHLEN, R. G. and COLLISTER, E. G. (1952): 'Sociometric status of sixth- and ninth-graders who fail to finish high school.' *Educ. and Psychol. Meas.*, 12, 632-7. **48, 53**

— and LEE, B. J. (1943): 'Personality characteristics and social acceptability in adolescence.' *J. Educ. Psychol.*, 34, 321-40. **44, 46, 85**

LANCELOT, W. H. (1935): 'A study of teaching efficiency as indicated by certain permanent outcomes', in Walker, H.M. (Ed.) (1935). **122**

LANZETTA, J. T. (1955): 'Group behavior under stress.' *Human Relations*, 8, 29-52. **80**

LATHAM, A. J. (1951): 'The relationship between pubertal status and leadership in junior high school boys.' *J. Genet. Psychol.*, 78, 185-94. **62**

LEEDS, C. H. (1950): 'A scale for measuring teacher-pupil attitudes and teacher-pupil rapport.' Psychological Monographs, No. 312, American Psychological Association.

LEWIN, K. (1947): 'Frontiers in group dynamics.' *Human Relations*, 1, 5-41 and 143-53. **6**

LIEBERMAN, S. (1956): 'The effects of changes in roles on the attitudes of role occupants.' *Human Relations*, 9, 385-402. **65**

LINDZEY, G. (Ed.) (1954): *Handbook of Social Psychology*. Cambridge, Mass.: Addison Wesley.

— and BORGATTA, E. F. (1954): 'Sociometric measurement', in Lindzey, G. (Ed.) (1954). **10**

LINS, L. J. (1946): 'The prediction of teaching efficiency.' *J. Exp. Educ.*, 15, 2-60. **122**

LIPPITT, R. and WHITE, R. K. (1943): 'The "social climate" of children's groups', in Barker, R. G., Kounin, J. S. and Wright, H. F. (1943): *Child Behavior and Development*. New York: McGraw-Hill. **57, 82, 104**

— — (1953): 'An experimental study of leadership and group life', in Newcomb, T. M. and Hartley, E. L. *et al.* (1947): *Readings in Social Psychology*. New York: Henry Holt.

LOBAN, W. (1953): 'A study of social sensitivity (sympathy) among adolescents.' *J. Educ. Psychol.*, 44, 102-12. **47**

LONGMORE, T. W. (1948): 'A matrix approach to the analysis of rank and status in a community in Peru.' *Sociometry*, 11, 192-206. **69**

LOOMIS, C. P. and PEPINSKY, H. B. (1948): 'Sociometry, 1937-1947: Theory and methods.' *Sociometry*, 11, 262-83. **10**

LOVELL, K. (1951): *An Investigation into Factors Underlying Teaching Ability in Primary and Secondary Modern Schools with a View to Improving the Methods of Selecting Potential Teachers.* Unpublished M.A. Thesis, University of London Library. **122, 124**

LUNDBERG, G. A. and BEAZLEY, V. (1948): ' "Consciousness of kind" in a college population.' *Sociometry*, 11, 59-74.

MCINTYRE, C. J. (1952): 'Acceptance by others and its relation to acceptance of self and others.' *J. Abn. and Soc. Psychol.*, 47, 624-5. **90**

MCLELLAND, F. M. and RATLIFF, J. A. (1947): 'The use of sociometry, as an aid in promoting social adjustment in a ninth grade home-room.' *Sociometry*, 10, 147-53. **47**

MANSKE, A. J. (1935): *The Reflection of Teachers' Attitudes in the Attitudes of Their Pupils.* New York: Teachers College, Columbia University.

MARTIN, W. E., DARLEY, J. G. and GROSS, N. (1952): 'Studies of group behavior: II. Methodological problems in the study of inter-relationships of group members.' *Educ. and Psychol. Meas.*, 12, 533-53.

— GROSS, N. and DARLEY, J. G. (1952): 'Studies of group behavior: Leaders, followers, and isolates in small organized groups.' *J. Abn. and Soc. Psychol.*, 47, 838-42. **62**

MARTINDALE, F. E. (1951): 'Situational factors in teacher placement and success.' *J. Exp. Educ.*, 20, 121-78.

MAYO, G. D. (1956): 'Peer ratings and halo.' *Educ. and Psychol. Meas.*, 16, 317-23.

MEAD, A. R. (1929): 'Qualities of merit in good and poor teachers.' *J. Educ. Res.*, 20, 239-59.

MEDLEY, D. M. and NITZEL, H. E. (1959); 'Some behavioral correlates of teacher effectiveness.' *J. Educ. Psychol.*, 50, 239-46.

MENSH, I. N. and GLIDEWELL, J. C. (1958): 'Children's perceptions of relationships among their family and friends.' *J. Exp. Educ.*, 27, 65-71. **70**

MORENO, J. L. (1934): *Who Shall Survive? A New Approach to the Problem of Human Relations.* Washington, D.C.: Nervous and Mental Disease Publishing Co. **9**

— (1937): 'Sociometry in relation to other social sciences.' *Sociometry*, 1, 206-19. **11**

— (1943a): 'Sociometry and the cultural order.' *Sociometry*, 6, 299-344.

— (1943b): 'Sociometry in the classroom.' *Sociometry*, 6, 425-8.

— (1946): 'Sociogram and sociomatrix.' *Sociometry*, 9, 348-9. **28**

— (1953): *Who Shall Survive? Foundations of Sociometry, Group Psychotherapy and Sociodrama.* New York: Beacon House. **8, 9, 10, 18, 68, 70**

— (1955a): 'The birth of a new era for sociometry.' *Sociometry*, 18, 261-8. **9**

Bibliography

MORENO, J. L. (1955b): 'The sociometric school and the ·science of man.' *Sociometry*, 18, 271-91. **10**

— and JENNINGS, H. H. (1938): 'Statistics of social configurations.' *Sociometry*, 1, 342-74. **31**

— — (1944): 'Sociometric methods of grouping and regrouping.' *Sociometry*, 7, 397-414.

— — (1945): *Sociometric Measurement of Social Configurations Based on Deviation from Chance*. Sociometry Monographs, No. 3. New York Beacon House. **36**

MORGAN, A. H. (1951): *A Study of Attraction and Repulsion within a Class-room*. Unpublished M.A. Thesis, University of London Library. **41**

MULLER, K. M. and BIGGS, J. B. (1958): 'Attitude change through undirected group discussion.' *J. Educ. Psychol.*, 49, 224-8. **76**

MYERS, C. C. (1916): 'The teacher's human frailties.' *Ped. Sem.*, 86-93. **102**

NATH, S. (1948): *An Investigation into the Significance of Teachers' Estimates of the Personal Attributes of Their Pupils for Secondary School Selection*. Unpublished M.A. Thesis, University of London Library. **108**

NEWMAN, F. B. and JONES, H. E. (1946): *The Adolescent in Social Groups. Studies in the Observation of Personality*. Stanford University Press.

NORTHWAY, M. L. (1940): 'A method for depicting social relationships by sociometric testing.' *Sociometry*, 3, 144-50. **22, 32**

— (1943): 'Social relationships among preschool children. Abstracts and interpretation of three studies.' *Sociometry*, 6, 429-33. **41, 61**

— (1944): 'Outsiders. A study of the personality patterns of children least acceptable to their age group.' *Sociometry*, 7, 10-25. **52, 55**

— (1946): 'Personality and sociometric status: a review of the Toronto studies. '*Sociometry*, 9, 233-41. **32**

— (1951): 'A note on the use of target sociograms.' *Sociometry*, 14, 235-6.

— and DETWEILER, J. (1955): 'Children's perception of friends and non-friends.' *Sociometry*, 18, 527-31. **50**

— FRANKEL, E. B. and POTASHIN, R. (1947): *Personality and Sociometric Status*. Sociometry Monographs No. 11. New York: Beacon House.

— and QUARRINGTON, B. (1946): 'Depicting inter-cultural relations.' *Sociometry*, 9, 334-9. **24**

NORTHWAY, M. L. and WIGDOR, B. T. (1947): 'Rorschach patterns related to the sociometric status of school children.' *Sociometry*, 10, 186-99. **47, 48, 90**

ODENWELLER, A. L. (1936): *Predicting the Quality of Teaching*. New York: Teachers College, Columbia University. **120, 122**

OJEMANN, R. H. and WILKINSON, F. R. (1939): 'The effect on pupil growth of an increase in teacher's understanding of pupil behavior.' *J. Exp. Educ.*, 8, 143-7.

OSTLUND, L. A. (1956): 'Group functioning under negative conditions.' *J. Educ. Psychol.*, 47, 32-9. **79**

PANTON, J. H. (1934): *The Assessment of Teaching Ability with Special Reference to Men Students in Training*. Unpublished M.A. Thesis, University of London Library. **122**

PARTRIDGE, E. D. (1943): 'The sociometric approach to adolescent groupings.' *Sociometry*, 6, 251-4. **3, 4, 5, 53, 59**

PEARCE, R. A. (1956): *Co-operation in the Classroom. A Study of a Form of Boys Working in Self-Chosen Groups of Friends in Several Subjects in Their First Two Years at a Grammar School*. Unpublished M.A. Thesis, University of London Library.

— (1958): 'Streaming and a sociometric study.' *Educ. Rev.*, 10, 248-51. **4, 54, 66, 79**

PEPINSKY, H. B., CLYDE, R. J., OLESEN, B. A. and VAN ATTA, E. L. (1952): 'The criterion in counselling: I. Individual personality and behavior in a social group.' *Educ. and Psychol. Meas.*, 12, 178-93.

PEPINSKY, P. N. (1949): 'The meaning of "validity" and "reliability" as applied to sociometric tests.' *Educ. and Psychol. Meas.*, 9, 39-49. **17**

PERKINS, H. V. (1951): 'Climate influences group learning.' *J. Educ. Res.*, 45, 115-19.

PHILLIPS, A. S. (1953): *An Examination of Methods of Selection of Training College Students*. Unpublished M.A. Thesis, University of London Library. **123**

PHILLIPS, B. N. and D'AMICO, L. A. (1956): 'Effects of cooperation on the cohesiveness of small face-to-face groups.' *J. Educ. Psychol.*, 47, 65-70. **77**

PHILLIPS, M. (1932): 'Some problems of adjustment in the early years of a teacher's life.' *Brit. J. Educ. Psychol.*, 2, 237-56. **117**

PORTER, W. A. (1942): 'Pupil evaluation of practice teaching.' *J. Educ. Res.*, 35, 700-4. **122**

POTASHIN, R. (1946): 'A sociometric study of children's friendships.' *Sociometry*, 9, 48-70. **3, 47, 49**

Bibliography

PRECKER, J. A. (1952): 'Similarities of valuings as a factor in selection of peers and near-authority figures.' *J. Abn. and Soc. Psychol.*, 47, 406-14. **50**

PRICE, L. (1940): 'Sociometric practices on the campus.' *Sociometry*, 3, 192-200.

PROCTOR, C. H. and LOOMIS, C. P. (1951): 'Analysis of sociometric data', in Jahoda, M., Deutsch, M. and Cook, S. W. (1951): *Research Methods in Social Relations. Part II. Selected Techniques.* New York: Dryden Press. **21, 24, 34, 36**

RASMUSSEN, G. R. (1956): 'An evaluation of a student-centered and instructor-centered method of conducting a graduate course in Education.' *J. Educ. Psychol.*, 47, 449-61. **75, 76**

RASMUSSEN, G. and ZANDER, A. (1954): 'Group membership and self-evaluation.' *Human Relations*, 7, 239-51. **6, 91**

REED, H. J. (1953): 'An investigation of the relationship between teaching effectiveness and the teacher's attitude of acceptance.' *J. Exp. Educ.*, 21, 276-325.

REYMERT, M. L. (1917): 'The psychology of the teacher: An introductory study.' *Ped. Sem.*, 24, 521-8. **112, 113**

RICHARDSON, J. E. (1948): *An Investigation into Group Methods of Teaching English Composition, with Some Consideration of Their Effects on Attainment and Attitude and a Sociometric Study of the Two Groups of Children Involved.* Unpublished M.A. Thesis, University of London Library. **75**

RICHARDSON, S. C. (1956): 'Some evidence relating to the validity of selection for grammar schools.' *Brit. J. Educ. Psychol.*, 26, 15-24. **107**

RINSLAND, M. A. O. (1938): 'A test for measuring teachers' knowledge of the conduct and personality of children from six to eight years of age.' *J. Exp. Educ.*, 6, 307-17.

ROBSON, M. M. (1918): 'An experimental study of character.' *J. Educ. Psychol.*, 9, 514-16. **96**

ROCCHIO, P. D. and KEARNEY, N. C. (1956): 'Teacher-pupil attitudes as related to nonpromotion of secondary school pupils.' *Educ. and Psychol. Meas.*, 16, 244-52.

ROSENTHAL, F. (1957): 'Some relationships between sociometric position and language structure of young children.' *J. Educ. Psychol.*, 48, 483-96. **43**

RUGG, H. (1921 and 1922): 'Is the rating of human character practicable?' *J. Educ. Psychol.*, 12, 425-38, 485-501, and 13, 30-42, 81-93. **86**

RUSSELL, H. E. and BENDIG, A. W. (1953): 'An investigation of the relationship of student ratings of psychology instructors to their course achievement when academic aptitude is controlled.' *Educ. and Psychol. Meas.*, 13, 620-35.

RYANS, D. G. (1951): 'A study of the extent of association of certain professional and personal data with judged effectiveness of teacher behavior.' *J. Exp. Educ.*, 20, 67-77. **124**

— (1952): 'A study of criterion data. (A factor analysis of teacher behaviors in the elementary school).' *Educ. and Psychol. Meas.*, 12, 333-44. **125**

— and WANDT, E. (1952a): 'Investigations of personal and social characteristics of teachers.' *J. Teacher Educ.*, Sept., 1952. **124**

— — (1952b): 'A factor analysis of observed teacher behavior in secondary schools.' *Educ. and Psychol. Meas.*, 12, 574-86. **125**

SANDERS, J. T. (1943): 'Sociometry and the sociology classroom.' *Sociometry*, 6, 249-50. **20**

SANDIFORD, P. *et al.* (1937): *Forecasting Teaching Efficiency*. Bulletin No. 8, Dept. of Educational Research, University of Toronto. **120, 122**

SEAGOE, M. V. (1942): 'Some origins of interest in teaching.' *J. Educ. Res.*, 35, 673-82. **115**

— (1946): 'Prediction of in-service success in teaching.' *J. Educ. Res.*, 39, 658-63. **122**

SHANNON, J. R. (1936): 'A comparison of three means for measuring efficiency in teaching.' *J. Educ. Res.*, 29, 501-8. **122**

SHEARS, L. W. (1952): *The Dynamics of Leadership in Adolescent School Groups*. Unpublished M.A. Thesis, University of London Library. **5, 60, 61, 62, 64, 66, 87**

SHEN, E. (1925): 'The validity of self-estimate.' *J. Educ. Res.*, 16, 104-7. **88**

SHERIF, M. and SHERIF, C. W. (1956): *An Outline of Social Psychology*. New York: Harper. **2, 5**

SHOOBS, N. E. (1946): 'Sociometric test in the classroom.' *Sociometry*, 9, 145-6. **60**

— (1947): 'Sociometry in the classroom.' *Sociometry*, 10, 154-64. **77**

SINGLETARY, J. (1951): 'Teacher-administrative leader perceptions of pupils.' *J. Educ. Res.*, 45, 126-32.

SHUKLA, J. K. (1951): 'A study of friendship', in Fleming, C. M. (Ed.) (1951). London: Routledge & Kegan Paul. **51**

SKINNER, W. A. (1949): *An Investigation into Assessment of Teaching Ability in Teachers of Technical Subjects*. Unpublished M.A. Thesis, University of London Library. **124**

SMALZRIED, N. T. and REMMERS, H. H. (1943): 'A factor analysis of the Purdue Rating Scale for Instructors.' *J. Educ. Psychol.*, 34, 363-7. **123**

SMITH, H. P. (1945): 'A study in the selective character of secondary education. Participation in school activities as conditioned by socio-economic status and other factors.' *J. Educ. Psychol.*, 36, 229-46. **45, 46**

— (1944): 'Some factors in friendship selections of high school students.' *Sociometry*, 7, 303-10. **50**

— (1946): 'Attitude homogeneity as a sociometric problem.' *Sociometry*, 9, 137-8. **6**

SOWER, C. (1948): 'Social stratification in suburban communities.' *Sociometry*, 11, 235-43. **50, 72**

SPRAGUE, H. A. (1917): 'Score-card for rating student-teachers in training and practice.' *Ped. Sem.*, 24, 72-80. **121**

STOGDILL, R. M. (1948): 'Personal factors associated with leadership: A Survey of the literature.' *J. Psychol.*, 25, 35-72. **58, 60, 62, 64**

STOTT, M. B. (1950): 'What is occupational success?' *Occupational Psychology*, 24, 105-12. **119**

SYMONDS, P. M. (1950): 'Reflections on observations of teachers.' *J. Educ. Res.*, 43, 688-96. **102, 106, 107**

TAYLOR, E. A. (1952): 'Some factors relating to social acceptance in eighth-grade classrooms.' *J. Educ. Psychol.*, 43, 257-72. **42, 43, 44**

TAYLOR, F. K. (1956): 'Awareness of one's social appeal.' *Human Relations*, 9, 47-56.

THOMSON, G. H. (1921): 'A rating scale for teaching ability in students.' *J. Exp. Ped.*, 6, 75-82. **120, 121**

THORPE, J. G. (1953): *A Sociometric Study of London Schoolchildren.* Unpublished Ph.D. Thesis, University of London Library. **31, 43, 48**

TIEDEMAN, S. C. (1942): 'A study of pupil-teacher relationships.' *J. Educ. Res.*, 35, 657-64. **112**

TOEMAN, Z. (1949): 'History of the sociometric movement in head-lines.' *Sociometry*, 12, 255-9. **8**

TORRANCE, E. P. (1954): 'Some practical uses of a knowledge of self concept in counselling and guidance.' *Educ. and Psychol. Meas.*, 14, 120-7. **93**

TRENT, R. D. (1959): 'Anxiety and accuracy of perception of socio-metric status among institutionalized delinquent boys.' *J. Genet. Psychol.*, 94, 84-91. **80, 91, 95**

TRIST, E. L. and SOFER, C. (1959): *Explorations in Group Relations.* University of Leicester Press. **57, 82**

TUDHOPE, W. B. (1942 and 1943): 'A study of the training college final teaching mark as a criterion of future success in the teaching profession.' *Brit. J. Educ. Psychol.*, 12, 167-71, and 13, 16-23. **122**
— (1944): 'Motives for the choice of the teaching profession by training college students.' *Brit. J. Educ. Psychol.*, 14, 129-41. **115, 116**
TYLER, B. B. (1958): 'Expectancy of eventual success as a factor in problem solving behavior.' *J. Educ. Psychol.*, 49, 166-72. **78**
UNIVERSITY OF LONDON INSTITUTE OF EDUCATION (1955): *Studies in Education. 7. The Bearings of Recent Advances in Psychology on Educational Problems.* London: Evans.
UTTLEY, G. W. (1952): *A Study of Some Aspects of Personality in Relation to Teaching Ability for a Group of Students in an Emergency Training College.* Unpublished M.A. Thesis, University of Birmingham Library. **123**
VALENTINE, C. W. (1934): 'An enquiry as to reasons for the choice of the teaching profession by university students.' *Brit. J. Educ. Psychol.*, 4, 237-59. **115, 116**
VERNON, M. D. (1937 and 1938): 'The drives which determine the choice of a career.' *Brit. J. Educ. Psychol.*, 7, 302-16, and 8, 1-15. **115**
VERNON, P. E. (1953): *Personality Tests and Assessments.* London: Methuen. **87**
VREELAND, F. M. (1942): 'Social relations in the college fraternity.' *Sociometry*, 5, 151-62.
WALKER, H. M. (Ed.) (1935): *The Measurement of Teaching Efficiency.* Kappa Delta Pi Research Publications. New York: Macmillan Company.
WALTERS, A. D. (1957): *An Investigation into the Value of Various Types of Information in the Selection of Training College Students and an Estimate of the Validity of Certain College Results.* Unpublished M.A. Thesis, University of Liverpool Library. **122, 123**
WERTHEIMER, R. R. (1957): 'Consistency of sociometric status position in male and female high school students.' *J. Educ. Psychol.*, 48, 385-90. **42**
WILKIE, J. S. (1955): *A Study of Some Effects of Free Choice of Certain Activities and Companions for Group Work of Junior School Children.* Unpublished M.A. Thesis, University of London Library. **77**
WILLIAMSON, E. G. and HOYT, D. (1952): 'Measured personality characteristics of student leaders.' *Educ. and Psychol. Meas.*, 12, 65-78. **61**
WITHALL, J. (1949): 'The development of a technique for the measurement of a social emotional climate in classrooms.' *J. Exp. Educ.*, 17, 347-61. **107**

WITHALL, J. (1951): 'The development of the climate index.' *J. Educ. Res.*, 45, 93-100.

— (1952): 'An assessment of the social-emotional climates experienced by a group of seventh graders as they moved from class to class.' *Educ. and Psychol. Meas.*, 12, 440-51.

— (1956): 'An objective measure of a teacher's classroom interactions.' *J. Educ. Res.*, 47, 203-12. **106**

WITHAM, E. C. (1914): 'School and teacher measurement.' *J. Educ. Psychol.*, 5, 267-78. **121**

WOLMAN, B. B. (1958): 'Education and leadership.' Teachers College Record, 59, 465-73. **4, 59**

WRIGHT, M. E. (1943): 'The influence of frustration upon the social relations of young children.' *Char. and Pers.*, 12, 111-22. **81**

WRIGHTSTONE, J. W. *et al.* (1952): 'An application of sociometric techniques to school personnel.' *J. Exp. Educ.*, 20, 301-4. **118**

WURSTER, C. R. and BASS, B. M. (1953): 'Situational tests: IV. Validity of leaderless discussions among strangers.' *Educ. and Psychol. Meas.*, 13, 122-32. **63, 85**

YATES, A. and PIDGEON, D. A. (1957): *Admission to Grammar Schools.* London: Newnes. **107**

YOUNG, L. L. (1947): 'Sociometric and related techniques for appraising social status in an elementary school.' *Sociometry*, 10, 168-77.

— and COOPER, D. H. (1944): 'Some factors associated with popularity.' *J. Educ. Psychol.*, 35, 513-35. **44, 47, 85**

ZELENY, L. D. (1940): 'Sociometry in the college classroom.' *Sociometry*, 3, 102-4.

— (1943): 'The value of sociometry in education.' *Sociometry*, 6, 247-8.

INDEX